Praise for *The Power of Love*

*"When we embrace the power of love, it cannot be extinguished.
Love is spirit."*

— **Deepak Chopra**, author of *Super Genes*

"The Power of Love *is a potent remedy for all that blocks our deepest yearnings
both to love and receive love. Filled with grounded truth, sage wisdom, and
profoundly healing energy—if you are ready to experience a transformational
shift and find freedom of fear and old habits, this book is for you. It will not
disappoint. It's a beautiful guide that I will embrace for my own journey."*

— **Sonia Choquette**, *New York Times* best-selling author of
The Answer Is Simple and *Ask Your Guides*

*"In his wonderfully profound book, James Van Praagh provides us with the
manual on how to tap into the essence of love. If you want to truly grow
and evolve, cultivate and share your innate gifts with others, and live a
more purposeful life—then this book is for you. James does a brilliant job in
demystifying our spiritual nature so that we can live more harmoniously
with others and ourselves. His knowledge and experience, so eloquently
written, combined with very practical tools will change your life.
I hope you enjoy it as much as I did."*

— **Dr. Joe Dispenza**, *New York Times* best-selling author of *You Are the Placebo*

*"James has created a masterful and easy-to-follow blueprint to navigate
our real-life challenges and awaken the magnificence resting in our heart."*

— **davidji**, author of *The Secrets of Meditation*

*"Guess what James Van Praagh has learned communicating with both dead people
and live ones? Love is the primary force of the universe whether from this side
or the other side. He has delicious insights about 'owning our love' and explores
questions and answers about love in this gem of a book. And he clearly shows how
love is the master healer. I believe you are going to love this book as I do!"*

— **Donna Eden**, author of *Energy Medicine* and *The Energies of Love*

THE
POWER
OF
LOVE

ALSO BY JAMES VAN PRAAGH

Books

*Adventures of the Soul**

How to Heal a Grieving Heart (with Doreen Virtue)*

Talking to Heaven

Reaching to Heaven

Healing Grief

Heaven and Earth

Meditations with James Van Praagh

Looking Beyond

Ghosts Among Us

Unfinished Business

Growing Up in Heaven

Card Decks

*The Soul's Journey Lesson Cards**

Talking to Heaven Mediumship Cards

(with Doreen Virtue)*

Online Courses

Adventures of the Soul

How to Heal a Grieving Heart*

Enhancing Your Intuition

Life After Loss

Mastering Meditation

Downloadable Meditations

Divine Love

Meditation Tools

Soul Discoveries

Spirit Speaks

*Available from Hay House

Please visit:

Hay House UK: www.hayhouse.co.uk
Hay House USA: www.hayhouse.com®
Hay House Australia: www.hayhouse.com.au
Hay House South Africa: www.hayhouse.co.za
Hay House India: www.hayhouse.co.in
James's website: www.vanpraagh.com

THE
POWER
OF
LOVE

Connecting to the Oneness

James Van Praagh

HAY HOUSE

Carlsbad, California • New York City • London
Sydney •Johannesburg • Vancouver • New Delhi

First published and distributed in the United Kingdom by:
Hay House UK Ltd, Astley House, 33 Notting Hill Gate, London W11 3JQ
Tel: +44 (0)20 3675 2450; Fax: +44 (0)20 3675 2451; www.hayhouse.co.uk

Published and distributed in the United States of America by:
Hay House Inc., PO Box 5100, Carlsbad, CA 92018-5100
Tel: (1) 760 431 7695 or (800) 654 5126
Fax: (1) 760 431 6948 or (800) 650 5115; www.hayhouse.com

Published and distributed in Australia by:
Hay House Australia Ltd, 18/36 Ralph St, Alexandria NSW 2015
Tel: (61) 2 9669 4299; Fax: (61) 2 9669 4144; www.hayhouse.com.au

Published and distributed in the Republic of South Africa by:
Hay House SA (Pty) Ltd, PO Box 990, Witkoppen 2068
info@hayhouse.co.za; www.hayhouse.co.za

Published and distributed in India by:
Hay House Publishers India, Muskaan Complex, Plot No.3, B-2,
Vasant Kunj, New Delhi 110 070
Tel: (91) 11 4176 1620; Fax: (91) 11 4176 1630; www.hayhouse.co.in

Distributed in Canada by:
Raincoast Books, 2440 Viking Way, Richmond, B.C. V6V 1N2
Tel: (1) 604 448 7100; Fax: (1) 604 270 7161; www.raincoast.com

A catalogue record for this book is available from the British Library.

ISBN: 978-1-78180-703-3

Printed and bound in Great Britain by TJ International Ltd, Padstow, Cornwall

To Brian.
Thank you for teaching me every day
how to use the power of love through
your actions, words, and presence.
I am eternally grateful.

CONTENTS

INTRODUCTION

*"Behind every veil I have drawn across the
face of love, its light remains undimmed."*

— A COURSE IN MIRACLES

Who am I? Where do I come from? Why am I
here? These are some of the most frequently asked
questions we throw out to the Universe, and few of us
seem to receive satisfying answers. If only we knew
why we come to Earth and what exactly our purpose
is, life would be so much easier to navigate. So, the
question remains: Why do we choose to come to a
place where war, hunger, hate, judgment, and the like
reign supreme? Why would we choose to be part of
an environment we cannot relate to, and where there
is little respect for each other? Why would any of us
choose to be in such an uncivilized world?

The answer is

♡ LOVE ♡

As a soul, you are part of a vast matrix of Universes within Universes that consists of millions, if not billions, of stars, planets, and solar systems. Souls traverse this great vastness, returning over and over into physical experiences as well as experiences on other stars and galaxies. Because your soul's journey is timeless, limitless, and immeasurable, it is unsurprising that you have forgotten who you truly are—a divine being of light. With each lifetime, you are given a fresh start for learning and a unique purpose to your life.

After meticulous pre-birth planning with your council of guides and teachers, you establish a curriculum for the life ahead of you in the schoolroom called Earth. Spirit guides are highly evolved beings that have completed their earthly incarnations. During spirit communication, I work with different spirit guides as sources of energy and expertise. The function of your guides is to assist and inspire you in your spiritual evolution. You are free to choose the situations, conditions, and other souls with whom you will share Earth time in order to have the greatest opportunities for spiritual growth. Experience isn't the only thing you seek; you have goals to meet, challenges to overcome, and proficiencies to perfect. Because we are souls learning to perfect our spiritual identities, many of us come to Earth with a desire to understand everything we can about jealousy, patience, forgiveness, anger, and the like. As souls, we share past karmic obligations that we want to clear up with other souls and even societies. It is the higher aspects of our intelligence that guide us into various life situations to allow our souls to choose the best paths to attain spiritual goals.

But why is it that we cannot remember our existence before Earth or the counsel given by our guides and teachers? As we reincarnate into the earthly vibration, we go through what is known as the Valley of Forgetfulness in order to start life with a clean slate. In Greek mythology, it is said that souls drink from the River Lethe (the river of forgetfulness) to lose all memory of their past existence.

Earth is a schoolroom, and there are some lessons that can be taught only here. These lessons are part of our everyday experiences; they are the "tests" we go through. If we knew all the answers to the tests beforehand, the lessons wouldn't be meaningful. Also, if a soul returned with a conscious memory of its "wrongdoings" or "right doings," it would waste valuable time obsessing over trying to make "right" the past and not live in the present. For instance, if we remembered how in a past experience we hurt someone or were hurt by someone, we might become fixated on the past and distracted from our soul's current curriculum. Yet, when we tune in to our soul through intuition and love, we can bring past-life experiences into the conscious mind if they are needed to learn our lessons. A soul comes back to heal an aspect of itself in order to bring more balance and harmony into its self-expression.

When our soul energy enters the physical vibration, it takes on the "limited" role of being a human and brings into play all the experiences from previous existences to form a personality. Our personalities continually expand or contract according to the amount of love we are willing to give and receive. As souls with bodies, we naturally work toward achieving human goals. But because we have a limited understanding of the soul's plan, we get caught up in the illusion of our three-dimensional world and come to believe that only the accumulation of material things and pleasures will bring true happiness. The further away a soul moves from its divinity and truth, the more it becomes centered in the "ego" and separated from its Source. We think of ourselves only as "material" beings, forgetting that we are "energetic" beings of light.

Within each soul is a vitality far greater than the fabric of the material world—it is the most powerful healing force that has ever existed. It can bring about wholeness from separation, balance from imbalance, and ease from disease, and can elevate emotions to levels of peace and joy. It is available to all, and yet used by so few. It is what we are made from and what we try so desperately to understand. It is the power of *love*—a power that is waiting for each and every one of us to put it to use. We need only to free ourselves from the self-imposed blocks of our limited egos to let this natural energy flow. Throughout the book, I offer solutions to the blocks and limitations we use to keep love away.

When we access love's energy, we open ourselves to the possibility of All That Is. Thus we experience the unlimited creative thrust of the Universe.

When I was eight years old, I experienced my first encounter with God's love. I was lying in bed and a cold gust of wind blew across my face. I looked up and saw a glowing hand of light above me. I wasn't afraid, because I felt peaceful and protected. I called this "hand of God" my guardian angel, and I knew I could count on it to help me. This same loving presence has guided me throughout my life to where I am today. Through this power of love, I have been able to communicate with the Spirit world to bring messages of comfort and spiritual insight to people everywhere I go.

Love resonates at the highest possible frequency. When we live at love's highest frequency, anything we desire will be met, for that is one of the characteristics of this power. The most difficult task with which we are presented is to maintain and bring forth *love* on a daily basis through all of our life experiences. This, my friends, is the main impetus for returning to our school called Earth.

When we use the power of love, we become aware of our place in our world and the cosmos beyond. We know our worth, and we value life and the lives of other living beings. We feel connected to one another as the light within us shines on everyone. We become divine messengers of the One Source, recognizing that we are not separate, but rather part of the Oneness of all life. With the power of love, we can live with contentment and true happiness. When we truly understand that we are here for spiritual growth, we can shift our perspective from that of a human consumed with earthly matters to that of a soul fueled by love.

With this perspective, not only do we benefit but so does the whole world.

I have divided the book into three parts. The first explains how we can love ourselves and share our love with others. The second sheds light on how we can use the power of love in making our everyday choices. And finally, the third shows how we can elevate our minds to cultivate an atmosphere of love, light, and joy. Included in this book are my own personal stories and those of people I have met on my journey. Each one demonstrated how they integrated the power of love and, by doing so, changed their entire view of life and its meaning. As you use this book, contemplate the solutions and let them help you expand your awareness of the power of love to bring a situation into wholeness and healing. Along with affirmations at the end of each solution, I have included meditations that will help you retrain your thinking.

Congratulations! You are about to take the first step toward bringing the energy of love into your life. I can't wait to share the many profound lessons there are about living your soul life. Before we dive in, here's one tip: as you travel along your own path to higher consciousness, it's helpful to be around like-minded people who also desire to live authentically, embrace love and gratitude, and raise the vibration of the planet.

May your heart be open to recognizing, remembering, and utilizing the divine power of love. Once love fills your life, neither you nor all those with whom you share life will be the same.

PART I

THE
ENERGY
OF LOVE

LOVING YOURSELF

"Everyone has to learn his or her particular lessons. All you can do is learn for yourself, and loving yourself is the first step."

— Louise Hay, *The Power Is Within You*

Your True Essence—Remembering Who You Are

Since my first book, *Talking to Heaven,* came out 20 years ago, I have been traveling the world, communicating with spirits, and spreading the knowledge of life after death in demonstrations, lectures, and workshops. I usually start off every workshop or lecture with: "You are a spiritual being having a human experience." Life here on Earth is a schoolroom, and while you inhabit a human body, your interactions with family, friends, lovers, co-workers, and strangers in all sorts of circumstances and situations are meant solely for the soul's learning.

Each one of us is made of the energy of divine light that is pure infinite love. The biggest illusion we have is that we see ourselves as being separate from one another. In love, we are not separate. That is why love is not something that you do; love is truly who you are. Love never left you and will never leave you; love is complete, constant, and immeasurable. Everything we experience in this life is meant to remind us that we are love. The question is: *What is holding you back from experiencing love in every moment of your life? What are you waiting for?*

As you reconnect to your soul, your priorities in life may change. You will discover that the answers to all your questions lie within your soul, not outside you. As I opened my mind to the power of love, I had many creative, forgiving, imaginative, and compassionate experiences. By constantly receiving impressions from Spirit, I learned how to distinguish my ego's fearful and insecure thoughts from the still, small voice of Spirit's love within me. I learned that by not judging my thoughts, no matter what they were, I was bringing more love into my awareness, and in doing so, I experienced more fun and freedom in my life.

Our earthly existence is just the tip of the iceberg—a speck of sand on the beach. When we realize that this life is just a fleeting moment in our soul's existence, it becomes clear that earthly concerns are merely illusions.

How Can I Perceive Myself beyond the Ego?

Your ego is your false self; it thrives on judgment, comparison, and guilt. It is your ego that always feels unhappy and unfulfilled. It is always comparing you to someone else. It projects unhappy thoughts and feelings out to the Universe and everyone around you. When you make choices from your ego, you are coming from your "Earth mind" and not your "Spirit mind," which is your true essence. Remember, the ego is the bridge between our true, spiritual self and our human self. It's necessary to have an ego in order to function on this human plane.

When my book *Adventures of the Soul* came out, I appeared on *The Doctors* TV show. I was asked to discuss soul-to-soul communication. When I speak of "soul-to-soul" communication, I am referring to the idea that the "mind" is an extension of the soul. The physical brain dies at physical death, but the soul/mind continues on, storing all memories and experiences of the just-lived life as well as previous and future lifetime experiences. When a spirit attempts to communicate with me as a medium, it projects a thought, feeling, or memory from its mind into my mind. This is soul-to-soul communication. I learned how to perfect my communication with the Spirit world by learning to surrender my own thoughts and putting my ego thoughts in a sort of state of suspension. Developing this ability took years of meditation and sitting in a development circle with like-minded individuals. Eventually, I was able to refine the skill to the point where I could create in my mind a blank screen upon which spirits could project their thoughts and feelings. When teaching mediumship to others, I often refer to spirit communication as the "mirror of the mind." A medium must surrender his or her mind space in order to be influenced by a spirit personality and present to the living any information as it is being experienced.

Dr. Jennifer Berman, the co-host of the show, volunteered as a subject. I quickly tuned in to her throat chakra and relayed that when she was between the ages of two and six, she couldn't express herself and her throat chakra closed down. By the time Dr. Berman was eight or nine, she was pushing herself intellectually to be more expressive—essentially telling herself something to the effect of *I have to get into my power and express myself.* I explained that she had blocked her self-worth. "You don't feel good enough. You don't feel worthy to be loved. You don't love yourself. You came back to learn about love—the many aspects of love. I believe this block could be from a past-life experience."

Dr. Berman admitted that she was blocked—it was hard for her to listen to the information I was giving her. She said that the one big area of her life that felt empty was not having a loving relationship. "I feel there is ice around my heart. I want to have hope that I'm not going to be left alone." Her mother in spirit came through to me and was adamant in communicating to her daughter to stop feeling insecure and unworthy. I told Dr. Berman that on an intuitive level, I didn't feel that she would be alone for the rest of her life, but I could tell that she could not shake off her fear. I said to her, "Fear is *false ego appearing real*. You're blocking yourself with fear. You have to put the energy of love out there to receive love back." Hearing my words and the words of her mother in spirit helped Dr. Berman gain a new perspective, but she still had much work to do on loving herself. She had to accept her weaknesses as equally as she accepted her strengths.

Dr. Berman's fear was one that she created. Like many of us, she excelled in achieving her material goals, but closed off the ability to express love to its fullest. The terror she felt at the thought of being alone had closed her heart to the love she sought. Whether you have everything life has to offer or very little, you have to feel worthy of being loved. If Dr. Berman could not love herself, how could she find someone else to love?

When things appear to be unreachable, know that this is an illusion of the ego. When you turn from your ego to your true self, strength, courage, and love will always guide you.

Solution: Self-Love

The most important goal you can achieve in this physical dimension is to love yourself unconditionally. You are the only one who can love you the way you need it, and also the only one who knows your secrets, faults, and shortcomings. It is so easy to take the lazy road and blame yourself for every flaw and failing. It's always easier to see the good in other people than in yourself. Do you really think you are the only person you know who is unworthy of your love? Only your ego thinks you are unworthy. The quality of love you give out is only as good as the quality of love you have for yourself. So stop shortchanging everyone by not loving yourself with the same intensity. In addition, the moment you begin to truly love who you are unconditionally and to live in that state, your life will change in very profound ways. The natural law of "like attracts like" applies here. Therefore, the people in your life who do not truly love you, but only pretend to, will be released from your life. Those who do indeed love you and are worthy of your love will remain. It is the Universe's way of bringing you to the truth.

I realize that love of self is necessary to love another.

How Can I Avoid Giving Away My Power?

Loving yourself means being true to yourself. You are not your mother, your father, your sibling, your spouse, or anyone else, so stop living the life they want you to and live your own life. Many of us find ourselves working to please someone in order to gain their love and affection. If we do this for any length of time, we tend to feel "less than" the other person. This lack of responsibility for our own happiness and worthiness can leave us feeling uncertain of our abilities, our values, and ourselves. We give away our power without even being aware of it. Often, our parents and spouses use guilt or shame to get us to do something for them. This only leaves us feeling angry and without control. If we push down these feelings, we will end up resenting those whom we say we love.

If you feel that you are constantly in situations where you need to defend yourself or your actions, you have placed too much importance on what other people think of you. Look at what you are doing to receive another's approval. Are you sacrificing a part of your wants and desires? If you are giving away your power in order to feel loved, you must begin to give yourself the same love you are willing to give another. You retain your power by making choices from your own free will. You cannot let someone else's words or actions trigger you into anger and attack. Be mindful that you are doing something because you want to do it. Be who you are and know that you are always enough.

There are so many ways we give away our power. It may start with little things and escalate to bigger, more emotionally disturbing behavior. Ruth, a friend of mine from college, was always planning her "perfect" future. She came from a family of attorneys and was following in the footsteps of her father and brothers. After getting her undergrad diploma in San Francisco, she went to New York University for her law degree. She was very focused on making all the right choices for her career; it was important to her that her family be proud of her accomplishments.

Ruth met the love of her life, Jesse, while attending law school; he was in pre-med coursework at Columbia. They moved in together, and Ruth felt everything was falling into place as it should—the right career, the right man, the right friends, and so on. She began a highly demanding job in the Brooklyn District Attorney's office, although it was a thankless position with very long hours. But she kept at it because she had promised Jesse that she would pay all his expenses while he attended med school and post-specialized training. I remember receiving an invitation to Ruth and Jesse's wedding with a note from Ruth—"Everything is working out so well. I am very happy."

Ten years passed, and although I hadn't kept in close touch with Ruth, when I was in New York to visit family I called her, and we arranged to have coffee and catch up. When I saw her, I was stunned. The years had not been kind to her; she looked haggard and emaciated. The only thing that remained the same was her smile. Naturally, I asked what was going on with her. It turned out that Jesse had not been the man of her dreams. After becoming a doctor, Ruth explained, "He became egotistical and narcissistic. He thought he was God's gift to women because the young nurses were throwing themselves at him."

By then Ruth was running herself ragged trying to please her boss at work and Jesse at home; she had little time for attending to her own needs. Ruth explained that one night when Jesse came home late, she asked him where he had been. "He got so enraged that I dared to ask him that he punched me in the face. It was the first time I saw the real Jesse." Ruth said she'd been too afraid to call the police. "I didn't want the neighbors to know, and I certainly didn't want anyone at work to find out." Unfortunately, Jesse took Ruth's silence as a sign of weakness, and so the battering continued.

When Ruth's sister found out what was going on, she helped Ruth find a safe haven. Eventually, Ruth got a divorce, but she carried the shame and guilt within her. She had a tough time facing the reality that she had given her power to someone else. She explained, "I kept getting mixed up with guys who were abusive, but thanks to my sister, I started seeing a therapist." My dear friend Ruth had to learn that she had to put her needs first without hurting anyone else. "That was very hard for me. I lived in a fantasy world with rose-colored glasses. It was a harsh lesson, to say the least."

Solution: Discernment

Ruth had to recognize the differences between love and fear, truth and illusion. Her choices had been based on what pleased others or what they wanted rather than on what she wanted. One of the hardest lessons is the art of discernment. When we use discernment on a daily basis, choices become natural. To be discerning, first, you must know yourself. As it says in *Hamlet*, "To thine own self be true, and it must follow . . . thou canst not then be false to any man." In other words, take care of yourself first so that you will be able to take care of others. When you are centered in your being and aware of your power, you are able to see the love and truth, as well as the falseness, in everyone. As you listen to others with a heightened awareness, you will hear between the words to what they really mean. Instead of making choices based on other people's opinions, honor who you are. Ruth had gone out of her way to please others and was so afraid of what others would think that she lost sight of her ability to make practical decisions that were right for her. When you honor yourself, you become aligned with your soul, and choices will be easier to make.

> I am developing the skill to distinguish love
> from fear and truth from illusion.

How Can I Restore My Power?

It seems much easier to give away our power than to get it back. Over the years, I have met many people who spend a lot of time revisiting their pasts, and specifically their childhoods. Having experienced abuse as a child is a prevalent theme. Childhood hurts can cause us to hold on to certain behaviors that no longer work for us in the present, and we often see the world with a distorted point of view. We have lost our power to recognize and follow our inherent self. To illustrate this, one woman in particular comes to mind.

Patricia came to my home when I first began private readings. She was middle-aged and had bright red hair. I remember her because, like the color of her hair, she was a ball of fire for such a tiny woman. As I tuned in to Spirit, Patricia was apprehensive and kept fidgeting in her seat. After I said my prayer and opened my eyes, she jumped up and walked around the room.

"Patricia, you will need to sit down and calm yourself," I said. "I am so nervous," she replied as she sat down. That was when I saw the figure of a woman wearing a long black dress with a white collar. At first, I was startled. She looked like a nun I'd seen as a child going to Sunday Mass. I began the reading. "There is a nun here." Before I could say anything else, Patricia jumped out of her seat again. I told Patricia that the nun was sorry for her behavior and that she wanted to be forgiven. Patricia returned to her chair and sat quietly through the rest of the reading. When I finished, Patricia was much calmer than when we began.

The nun had been cruel to Patricia with her put-downs and bullying. It was not an unusual state of affairs; many people taught by nuns in Catholic schools have had similar experiences. The twist was that the nun came through to ask for forgiveness. Several months later, I received a letter from Patricia that I still have. Sharing her thoughts, Patricia wrote, "I was so afraid of making mistakes because I could hear Sister Bernadette's voice chastising me for doing it wrong . . . I lived in fear most of the time. I always had a hard time making decisions. Most of the time

I waited too long, and opportunities came and went. You might say I was reborn that afternoon because the fear is now gone. I no longer need to give it any more of my time and thoughts. I can't thank you enough for changing my life."

Solution: Responsibility

Unfortunately, Patricia had lived most of her life looking behind her to see if Sister Bernadette was waiting to criticize and condemn her. Throughout my years as a medium, I cannot tell you how many people I've met who have been enslaved by their past relationships, unable to forgive and move on. The past has no power over us unless we give it power in our minds. The best way to let go of the past is to see it as a teacher and send love to all those who have hurt you and whom you have hurt.

When we let go of the past, we can direct the wisdom we learned from those experiences and demonstrate our individual soul expression. In other words, we can take back our power and become responsible for our lives. In Patricia's mind, she could never live up to Sister Bernadette's standards. Because she acted from the need for the approval and acceptance of others, she took on the role of victim and was unable to make up her own mind. No matter what her faults or secrets were, it was time for her to take control of her actions. Fortunately, Patricia was able to let go of the past and head in the direction where she could create a reality that was uniquely her own.

> I am aware of the power of my thoughts
> and the amount of love I am able to express.

Love or Fear

Like Patricia, most of us are reticent to take charge of our lives because we live in uncertainty. But there are really only two ways we can experience life— through love or through fear. That's it. You are where you are in your life because of the countless choices you have made based on these two responses. Do you know which choices were based on fear, lack, and insecurity? Did you choose the school or career that your parents desired because you wanted to please them? Or did you listen to your soul and follow the beat of your own drum? Fear is very powerful; it can overwhelm any positive tendency we may work toward.

Because of fear, most people tend to be reactive and judgmental instead of being proactive and loving. We judge others because we want more control over our lives, or we build an energetic wall around ourselves that keeps others at arm's length. This may be an unconscious way of protecting ourselves from being hurt, especially if we have been hurt in the past. Every soul goes through various degrees of hurts in the human lifetime. It seems that hurt is a vital lesson in the awareness of the soul's power.

In order to release the negative energy of fear, we must look to see where fear resides in our lives. The energy of fear takes on many guises—anger, hate, resentment, judgment, shame, and guilt—and fosters feelings of low self-worth and a lack of self-respect. Living in fear stops our natural flow of vitality and brings forth emotional, mental, and physical traumas and upheavals.

Treat yourself like you would your dearest friend. If a friend shared a mistake he made at work, you wouldn't say, "How could you be so stupid?" Instead, you would remind him of his good qualities and per-haps say, "You'll do better next time." You would reassure your friend that he is a valuable person, dear, and precious not only to you but also to others. Would it be so terrible to say these things to yourself?

As a teacher, I am always illustrating how the power of love can help you transcend fear and change any life circumstance into a learning situation. To incorporate love into every aspect of your life, you will have to retrain your way of thinking into mindfulness, gratitude, forgiveness, and compassion. Use the meditations and affirmations in this chapter daily to guide your new way of thinking.

Be honest with yourself. Become aware of your thoughts and feelings. At the same time, stop judging yourself. If you do get fearful, critical, or upset, don't fight yourself or make matters worse by adding guilt to the other feelings. Release your inner conflict and know that everything in your life is there for a reason, no matter how unpleasant it seems to be at the time.

Setting Your Sacred Space

To embrace the power of love, take the time to be still every day. It is in the silence that you can communicate with your soul's needs and understanding. I can never give enough credit to the art of meditation, prayer, or contemplation—to me, these terms are interchangeable. Take time every day to meditate. As I say to my students, *Meditate, meditate, meditate!*

Meditation will help you put a period at the end of each thought so you can let the thought move on. Pick a time and a place where you can sit quietly and comfortably and focus on your breath. Thoughts will come and go; don't worry about the inner chatter. There will be little gaps between the thoughts, and with practice these gaps will expand. Over time, you will find that you are less stressed and more aware of the present moment.

When the mind is clear, you can hear the truth. Whatever method you use, the key is to bring yourself to the silence and listen to the yearnings of your soul. It is normal for the human mind to wander and get caught up in its judgments and criticisms. Just make a conscious choice to observe the judgment and then let it go with no attachment. In this way, you don't give it any undeserved power. The more you practice the stillness of being, the easier it will be to focus on the *nothingness*. It is within this void of nothingness that you will receive the most profound insights.

MEDITATION—SELF-LOVE

In your mind's eye, imagine yourself walking along a beautiful garden path. You are creating a reality with your imagination that you call your True

World. It is yours alone because you design everything in it. Here in your True World are the sights, smells, sounds, and touches that nurture you, that comfort your senses. With each inhalation of your breath, allow yourself to go deep within the inner aspects of your soul. With each exhalation, give yourself permission to release cloudy, limiting thoughts, stifled emotions, and stagnant energy.

Become conscious of the space at the top of your head where the imagination resides. This is the "screen of your mind." Slowly and gently place yourself within the screen of your mind. With each breath, allow a new, pure, healing thought to enter and let each new thought balance out any stray negative thought. Gently glide each foot along the path in becoming totally aware of your True World. Float above the ground easily and naturally. With each loving thought, the terrain you float above becomes activated with your energy. You notice flowers along your path, and with each gliding motion, the flowers awaken. As if in perfect rhythm with your step, each petal of each flower slowly opens, releasing a brilliant and dazzling light.

Feel the strength of life as the light and color illuminate the path below you. Your thoughts respond to this magnificent beauty with gratitude and appreciation. Each thought you give is immediately returned to you as a compliment. In your True World, all giving is receiving. With each breath, the path extends outward to form one majestic garden covered with flowers and grasses of incredible hues, textures, and shapes. Nothing is disturbed as you float above the garden. The sensation of being totally free yet at one with everything astounds you.

The flowers speak in your mind: "We are reflections of your soul. All you are seeing is the love inside you!" There is no place for self-criticism or blame, because you are pure like the flowers. All self-judgment comes from your ego, not your True World. The flowers reflect the beauty within you. Once you begin to realize how beautiful and loving you truly are, you will want to share your love with the world around you. It is so easy to love others and for others to love you, but first you have to remember who you *truly* are. The human space called Earth has struggles for the ego, but in your True World, love of the self is the natural state. You always have the ability to enter your True World and center your focus here. This is home.

As you breathe in and out gently, begin to bring your thoughts back to your body. Fill it with the sunshine of your new awareness. Slowly open your eyes, and share the beauty of your self-love with everyone who walks upon your human path.

2

WAYS TO GROW AND EVOLVE

"When you are full of problems, there is no room for anything new to enter, no room for a solution."

— ECKHART TOLLE, *THE POWER OF NOW*

Seeing from Another Point of View

Everywhere I go, I see auras, beautiful light that surrounds people. This beautiful light represents the potential that exists in them that they don't see in themselves. (I will explain more about auras in Chapter 4.) With all the information that comes through from the Spirit world, you might think I could tell people what to do, how to behave, and what would be best for them. However, in the past 30 years of giving messages, I've learned a very important lesson: you can never control another person or their behavior. It's one thing to give advice, but another thing to take it. The Spirit world may assist me in presenting something to a person in a different way, but it is not up to me to live their life or make choices for them. The simple truth is that each of us is the creator of the world we are experiencing, and everyone on our path is there for a reason.

When I was doing my show *The Ghost Whisperer* years ago in Hollywood, I worked with many wonderful, creative people, along with some I am glad not to have to deal with again. I remember befriending Stephanie, one of the production assistants on the show, who dreamed of one day producing her own television series. At the time, she was in charge of making sure that our production staff was taken care of by bringing them coffee, the daily script changes, and whatever else they needed to facilitate their jobs. She was a happy, kind, and creative person, but underneath the smiles, I could sense her insecurity.

After we had known each other for a while, Stephanie confided in me about an incident that had made her quite upset. As she told me her story, her tears came to the surface. "I had this script that I was going to present to the network executives. Before I did, I gave it to a good friend and asked him to give it to one of the producers he was working for. I thought he would help me get my foot in the door and we could work on the show together." I was starting to feel the direction this story was taking. "Behind my back, my friend gave it to the network and didn't include me in the presentation. I was heartbroken that he could betray me like that. I guess you can't trust anyone in this business, not even your friends." Then her emotion turned to anger. "I'm going to be ruthless, and lie and cheat like everyone else."

I shook my head. "Don't lower yourself to their level," I said. "Always take the high road. I know you will succeed, but you have to do it your way. Raise others up with your love and kindness. It will pay off for you." It's unfortunate that people are greedy and hurtful and behave in unethical ways, but we must look at each situation from a higher perspective and see it as a lesson we chose to learn. No matter the situation, only we can label it as "good" or "bad," and only we can change our point of view about the experience. Until Stephanie was willing to reevaluate the situation from a different point of view, her feelings of bitterness and regret would fester and grow. Remember that we have come to Earth school with a plan, and what we think of as a failure may actually be a turning point that will take us to where we need to be.

What Can I Do to Replace Limitations and Faults?

I often tell my audiences to reconcile any differences they may have with others while they are still in the physical world, because we carry our unfinished business into the next world. We have many more opportunities to resolve conflicts in the earthly sphere than we do in Spirit. When you can release a misunderstanding, mistake, or fault here in the world by forgiving the other person, no matter what pain or hurt he or she may have caused, you expand the love in your heart. Forgiveness provides an incredible feeling of empowerment and freedom. When you forgive another, you are forgiving yourself at the same time.

When I first started doing readings at home, a woman came to me because she had lost her husband. I began the session and could sense her husband's spirit immediately because he was very anxious to talk. I put my hands on my head and felt like I was spinning in circles. "I can tell your husband was disoriented when he passed over. He was out of control. Do you understand?" She revealed that her husband had been an alcoholic: "He died in a car crash after blacking out behind the wheel." I continued, "Your husband is telling me that he is sorry that he didn't have a good relationship with you. He was always thinking of himself. Now, he says, he is aware that what he did had a terrible effect on you. He says he put you through hell, and that he's come here to heal the relationship with you as best he can." I told the woman, "You know, he's around you all the time now—something he didn't do when he was alive."

The woman let out a sigh of relief. She told me that she'd felt it was her fault. "I thought I could help him, but I couldn't stop him from drinking. I felt so foolish and so guilty that I couldn't keep my own husband from drowning in booze." She went on to admit that she had been feeling very depressed and had started to drink too much herself. "But now I feel I can put my shattered life together—I have hope."

Because spirits live in a world that vibrates at a much higher level than our human world, their feelings and thoughts are amplified. What they create with their thoughts, words, and actions is more vivid, maybe 10 or 20 times more intense, than while they are on Earth. Because this man's uncaring attitude was magnified on the other side, it was clear to him how badly he had behaved, and he felt genuine remorse. I sensed that the communication allowed the couple to heal very deep wounds. They were very fortunate; in other cases, I have seen those in Spirit who were unable to release their mistakes and took their regrets into future lives.

After the reading, I suggested that the woman write her husband a letter expressing her love and forgiveness. "You have to accept what was and not be a victim of the past." I also suggested that she get help with her drinking and release her self-condemnation so she would not become a victim of faults and limitations, like her husband had.

Solution: Acceptance

When we stay in a relationship because it would be a hassle to leave or not in our best interest financially, we show how little we value ourselves when we don't even make an effort to change what is not working. It might be easier to nurse our hurt feelings and replay scenes where we could have acted differently. Like the woman above, we can spend a lifetime looking back at our regrets. Changing what we've gotten used to can be challenging. Because life is unpredictable and impermanent, it will present many obstacles to test us. We will progress faster when we accept the twists and turns life affords us.

Learning to accept adversity and adapting to what is—whether it is a family loss, a missed opportunity, or an unexpected change in plans—will help you maintain a sense of inner peace. So many of us say that we want to find inner peace, and yet we seem to find inner turmoil. The same is true of love. We say we want love, but we spend most of our time judging ourselves and others. Love and peace are interchangeable. When you are peaceful, you feel love, and when you feel love, you are peaceful.

When you look at any situation, instead of being confused or worried about what to say or do, let love and peace be your guides. Acceptance is the way to see life objectively. We are not in control of one another's behavior, nor are we bound by one another's behavior. Even when we accept what is happening, we can still choose another outcome. Allow yourself the freedom to be yourself, accept what you can change and what you cannot, and move on.

I am now ready to release control of situations and observe without judgment the unique rhythm of everyday life.

How Can I Honor My God-Given Gifts?

We have often heard it said that God gives us only as much as we can handle, and as disturbing as an experience may be, souls always have the aptitude and abilities to handle whatever they originally signed up for.

Several years ago, I met a woman on one of my spiritual cruises. She wasn't there as part of my group, but she was very friendly and curious about the work I did and the people with me. I noticed the beautiful shawl she was wearing and asked her where she had gotten it. The woman, Mary Ann, replied, "Oh, I didn't buy it, I made it myself. I make a lot of shawls like this, and many other things." So we began talking. Mary Ann was probably one of the most extraordinary people with whom I had ever crossed paths. The oldest of 10 children from a poor farming family, she was responsible for getting her brothers and sisters up and ready for school, preparing breakfast, cleaning the house, doing the laundry, and making dinner at night when her father came in from the fields. Her mother was an alcoholic, and unable to handle chores or children. When her father died suddenly of heart failure, Mary Ann's mother could not cope with the responsibility of managing the farm, so Mary Ann took charge.

"Everyone got a chore to do, and we were able to keep the land and the house." In between taking care of the cows and farming the land, Mary Ann sewed all the clothes for her brothers and sisters. They were not the usual farmhand-type clothes, and people in town took notice. "I started making clothes for neighbors, and it soon turned into a very nice business." Mary Ann's creativity and financial savvy helped the farm grow and prosper. She was able to hire others so she could focus on designing and selling her collection of clothing and accessories. "What did you do with your success?" I asked. Mary Ann responded, "We shared it." I looked at her: "How?" "I wanted to help people like my mother, so we built a house on the land as a sober home. It was free to anyone who needed help." Mary Ann teaches us all to honor our talents and lend a helping hand.

Solution: Humility

At a young age, Mary Ann developed a loving awareness that everyone is the same, only on different paths. Through her compassion, she accepted her mother's frailty and imperfections. At the same time, she was able to fulfill the many needs of her family with love and without complaint. Although she faced many trials and obstacles, she took a chance with new ideas that not merely benefited, but also enhanced the welfare of all involved.

Humility allows us to be conscientious and compassionate with each other. We feel true joy from giving rather than receiving. We are grateful for what life has presented to us and enthusiastic for what tomorrow may bring. When we live without self-importance and pride, like Mary Ann did, we find it easier to practice kindness. We realize that life revolves around not only what we can do to succeed but also what we can do to help those we encounter along our path. As humble souls, we don't compare ourselves to others because we realize that it is our uniqueness that teaches that everyone has a purpose for being.

I am developing the loving awareness
that everyone is the same, only on different paths.

How Do I Keep My Heart Open?

I firmly believe that every soul who walks upon your path is doing so for a very specific reason: you are either learning an aspect of love from that person or sharing another way for the person to look at him- or herself.

At a class at the Omega Institute for Holistic Studies, a spiritual learning center in Rhinebeck,

New York, I was sitting on the cafeteria patio during a lunch break when a woman's loud voice boomed overhead, asking if she could sit down next to me. The voice belonged to Nancy, an Omega faculty member who taught a writing class on campus. She was not only hysterically funny but also very down-to-earth. I don't remember how we got on the subject, but she told me about an experience that I will probably never forget. Many years earlier, Nancy had read one of her student's poems and been amazed that it was so good, beyond her expectations. She told the student, who happened to be 96 years old, that her poetry had to be published. The old woman, Tess, looked at her teacher with tears in her eyes and said, "I just wanted to be famous my whole life, but it never happened!" Nancy told Tess, "Leave it to me." In a series of phone calls and e-mails, Nancy contacted her friend at a publishing company and the two decided Tess's poems would be great published as a coffee-table book.

After many years of merging beautiful photographs with Tess's poetry, the book was published. The photographs honored the words, and several actresses, including Mary Steenburgen, gave poetry readings at local bookstores. The day before Nancy brought Tess to her first reading, the old woman turned 106 years old! At the reading, Tess grasped Nancy's hand and, with tears in her eyes, said, "Thank you." Nancy went way out of her way to make sure this woman's dream came true. The old woman—happy, content, and complete at last—passed quietly the next day.

Solution: Friendliness

If it weren't for the kindness and friendliness of Nancy, an old woman may have passed into the Spirit world holding regrets over a life unfulfilled, and I would not have had the opportunity to share Tess's story with you.

Opening your heart to others without any expectation of reward or conditions to be met is a clear indication that you are excited to meet new people and share in different experiences. Friendships afford us opportunities to show our vulnerabilities, so that together we can learn and grow. No one comes into your life by accident. The more you send forth the energy of friendliness, the more it continues to charge the atmosphere around you and anyone with whom you come into contact. Friendliness mitigates the possibility of creating a negative karmic tie. We are always being presented with lessons for our spiritual evolution. Karma is a tool for learning—we can create positive or negative karma by responding with love or fear, friendliness or irritation. We are all in this world together for support and encouragement. Simply start with a smile.

> I recognize common traits in others and
> appreciate the connections of love.

Is It Possible to Tune In to Spirit?

The experiences in this physical dimension, with all its struggles and obstacles, seem very real to us. Our awareness of love is constantly filtered through our human senses. If we understood that the lessons of our Earth journey are to teach us to become aware of our divine birthright and to wake up from the illusion of our physical identity, life would take on a completely different meaning. That is why we reincarnate. As we learn, we evolve. However, becoming aware and seeking our spiritual identity doesn't mean that we have to sacrifice our human needs. We are all worthy of succeeding, even if we are 106 years old.

When I started opening to Spirit, I knew I had to share my information about life after death. At the time, I lived in a small apartment, and as my clientele grew, I rented a charming Craftsman home in

West Hollywood. I hired an assistant to take calls and schedule appointments. I was working independently and was solely responsible for my income. Although it was exciting and scary at the same time, I knew that Spirit was pulling strings that would dramatically change my life.

I made my first television appearance in 1994 on a show called *The Other Side*. Very soon after, I became a semi-regular on the show. From then on, my phone rang off the hook with people asking for readings. One day Larry King's producer called. She'd seen me on *The Other Side* and asked if I had a gimmick. (*Larry King Live* was a popular TV show on CNN from 1985–2010.) I said, "I talk to dead people, isn't that enough?" She said, "Sorry," and that was that. Two years later, I wrote a book about my experiences, *Talking to Heaven*. Dutton, my publisher, didn't have much faith in the book because the subject matter was new and unusual.

Since the publisher wasn't doing much to promote it, I knew in my heart that it was my job to get the book out there. I decided to call Larry King's producer and tell her that my first book was just published. While I was speaking, the spirit of her grandfather appeared to me. He said, "Tell her that her mother is taking too many pills, and that she has my glasses in the second drawer in the nightstand by the bed." I repeated those words to the producer, and she immediately booked me on the show. That Friday night after the show's airing, CNN bureaus around the world were swamped with calls for me. My book went from a printing of 6,000 copies to well over 600,000 copies in the following weeks. The Spirit world made sure to get the message out.

Spirits can help from the other side, but they can never directly interfere in the natural development of events. In this particular instance, the love of a grandfather influenced the love of his granddaughter, and as a result, I appeared on the show with a message of love that helped many others.

Every soul has embedded in it a unique stamp and a distinct purpose. There was no way that people could stop me from doing what Spirit wanted me to do. None of us knows what the Universe has planned for us. Everything that happens is part and parcel of a bigger picture, and each of us has chosen a part to play. Our job is to trust in Spirit. When we let go of our egos and surrender to the love within us, we open the space for Spirit to manifest miracles in our lives.

Solution: Trust

When you listen to your soul's voice, you will not travel a path that is not meant for you. To access the voice of your soul, you must turn down the noise and static of everyday life, even if only for a few minutes each day. You can do this by meditating, journaling, or taking a quiet, mindful walk. Give yourself permission to sense the energy of your soul being. Practice this every day, and you will find your connection to your own inner awareness expanding. As with learning anything new, you must study and practice to become more proficient. When you tune in to that still, small voice of the soul, you honor the knowledge it imparts by acting on it. Remember that the voice of Spirit never judges or condemns. It is the voice of love. Love is the great creator. Even when several publishers rejected my book, I trusted in Spirit. Every time I faced an obstacle, I knew it was another learning opportunity. I knew the love my book contained had to be experienced by the world. The more you trust the voice of Spirit, the more easily you can flow through life. You will look at challenges as opportunities and trust that you can adapt and change. Regardless of how people and circumstances present themselves to you, when you follow the voice within, you will feel a sense of inner peace.

I have a strong connection to my soul's loving voice.

MEDITATION—ACCEPTANCE

Close your eyes and gently become mindful of each inhalation and exhalation. With each inhalation you are telling the Universe that you are ready to receive its nurturing energy to bring you strength, health, balance, and clarity. With each exhalation, you are releasing to the Universe all thoughts, energies, and behaviors that hold you back from accepting your true, loving self.

Now imagine that all of your awareness is concentrated in a single beam of light. Begin to scan your inner body with this light. This beam of light will guide you to areas in the body where conflict or imbalance live. As you observe each of these areas, your intuition will immediately let you know why there is a disruption in the energy flow. Your body is a tuning fork for the world around you, and it directly responds to your thoughts. Does the source of this imbalance derive from an emotional, mental, physical, or spiritual memory or experience in your past? Why is it creating conflict? Is your inner self at the same energy level as the outer world you perceive right now? Are you opposed to any events that are now happening in your life?

As you scan this area, ask yourself if there is some part of yourself that you are not accepting. What is in conflict with your true self and the outer world? Are you attempting to live a life that is not yours just to be accepted and loved by someone else? What are you learning from this stagnation? The light illuminates your mind and you are given the choice to free yourself from this pain and release it. If something makes you unhappy, it does not belong to you, and you freely give it up and let your energy flow effortlessly. Your natural inner environment is happiness, balance, and peace. Your natural state of being is love. Accept yourself.

3

SHARING LOVE WITH OTHERS

"When we know that we are love, we don't need to work at being loving toward others."

— ANITA MOORJANI, *DYING TO BE ME*

Sharing the Energy of Love through Relationships

Many people wish for love and find that it eludes them. We can't just wish for love. We have to own love in ourselves. Wishing and hoping for love only signifies that you doubt that love is real and that it is real for you. Before you can truly love or be loved by someone else, you have to know that you are love. In order to attract love, you must be loving. If you find fault with yourself, you certainly will find fault with someone else. You don't have to be perfect to find a great relationship. Just know that the other person will mirror to you what you see in yourself. You're a human being that inhabits a human body, and as George Carlin once said, you have "stuff"! Yes, we all have "stuff"!

If you are seeking your one special soul mate, be patient. The Universe will send you the perfect person meant just for you; it just might take a little time. In the meantime, enjoy creating and sending loving energy to the world by performing small acts of kindness for friends, family, strangers, and animals. Every day, I make it a mission to change the energy around at least one person to demonstrate the loving parts of each of us. Love is never to be kept locked away—it grows only by sharing.

Years ago I had the chance of a lifetime to paddle an outrigger canoe with several other people off the coast of Tahiti. In order to propel ourselves through the water, we had to row in unison. I thought, *Simple*. But as a beginner, I found myself distracted by the scenery, watching for dolphins, and focusing too much on everyone in the boat. Needless to say, my lack of attention caused my paddle to clunk and splash, and the canoe seemed to be fighting its way through the water. I asked the steerer, "How do I do this the right way?" He told me to focus on putting my oar in the water at the same time as the paddler in front of me. When everyone was rowing in unison, I would feel the flow. Sure enough, I focused on the area right in front of my oar, and soon the boat was gliding effortlessly through the water—I felt the flow!

The same is true of relationships. If we can flow with each other instead of going against the current, life becomes more harmonious. Relationships afford us the best opportunities to learn and grow as spiritual beings. But learning is never easy, and relationships often take us out of our comfort zones. We are here to understand all sides of an experience, and the hardest part to comprehend is that we have no control over other people's behavior and actions.

Can I Let Go of Hurt and Sadness?

Every one of us has been in and out of love throughout life. Young lovers think they can never live without one another, and they become enamored of human attention and attachment. But when romantic love starts to fade and the bloom is off the rose, many relationships come to an end. Interests change, situations evolve, and people find other lovers. Naturally, there is a lot of pain when a breakup happens. You miss your partner, and inevitably everything reminds you of him or her. The hurt is agonizing. This was the story of my friend's daughter, Sara, who went through just such a breakup.

Sara had been married for six years and was successful in her career. Like many women, she had waited to have children, and when the timing seemed right, she and her husband decided to start a family. Unfortunately, she couldn't get pregnant and underwent in vitro fertilization. A year went by, and still Sara couldn't conceive. Then one day, she walked into her home office and noticed that her husband had left his Facebook page open. She read through the entries and saw something curious. He was having many conversations with a certain colleague at work. One thing led to another, and she found out that her husband had been having an affair while she was trying to get pregnant. Needless to say, she was devastated. At first she was so hurt, she couldn't think straight, so she stopped working. Eating and sleeping were difficult. She begged her husband to go to couple counseling. "After all," Sara pleaded, "we're planning a family." Reluctantly, her husband agreed, and for the next year, the two seemed to be back on track. They discussed their fears, anxieties, anger, and disappointments with their therapist, who gave them guidelines and advice. In the end, however, they couldn't come to a happy solution, so they parted ways. The husband went off with his new love, and Sara fell into a state of bitterness and rage. She started sending hateful e-mails to her ex-husband and his girlfriend. She wanted him to feel the hurt she felt. Her anger and hate spilled out onto family and friends, and eventually they stayed away from her. Finally, anger turned into depression and Sara thought about killing herself.

With the help of her therapist, Sara realized that her feelings of loss and abandonment could make her stronger. Once she went through the stages of grief—from shock, denial, anger, guilt, and depression to acceptance—Sara began to love herself again. She learned not to expect someone else to fill up her life with love. Sara's soul waited for her to see the light of her true nature.

Sara eventually moved away and went back to school to earn a teaching credential. Presently, she works in special education helping handicapped children, and, according to my friend, she is happier in her new career than she had been in her previous one. Sometimes, our greatest adversities force us to go deep within our souls to find the love and strength necessary to succeed. Sara's dream of having children was answered, but in the way she least expected.

Solution: Forgiveness

The next time you find yourself replaying an old grievance, think about what you learned from having the experience. Remember that it's your ego that is bruised, not your soul. Maybe you needed to become aware of a recurring theme. Like Sara, you could be attracting a pattern of being rejected. Or perhaps it was a past-life karmic obligation that you had to meet, balance, and live out. Once you determine what you have learned from the situation, give yourself permission to grieve, forgive, and move on.

Forgiveness is the cornerstone of love—it is a gift you give yourself. To be aligned with the power of love, complete forgiveness of yourself and the other person is necessary. Be willing to release hurt, revenge, and resentment—they only cloud love and prevent it from entering your life. It is in your forgiving that healing takes place. Send the other person your love and gratitude for assisting you in learning the lesson, and then release it. It is important that you forgive, but not necessarily forget. Don't stuff down your feelings, but don't wallow in them either. Forgiveness is for you, not the other person. When you say, *I forgive you*, you are telling yourself, *I free myself from any pain regarding this situation*. My grandmother used to say, "Write it on the ice!" which was her way of telling me to forgive and move on.

I activate the power of love in order to release past hurts and to accelerate my spiritual evolvement.

How Can I Attract Loving People into My Life?

Once we let go of what was, we open the door to what can be. And yet there are many people who have never experienced the intimacy of having a loving partner. My friend Anna is a gentle soul who surrounds herself with cats that she has rescued. Unfortunately, she has no clue about sharing the love she has for her cats with another human. In her mind, the cats give her all the love she will ever need, and she has resigned herself to that fact. When I asked her why she did not want to go out and meet people, she replied, "Why would I want to subject myself to *that*?" "That" was her way of saying: *I don't want to be rejected.* Anna's cats can't reject her because they rely on her care, and so she is content with the love of her cats.

My friend Kevin, a gay man, never had a loving partner. As he said to me, "I have been looking for Mr. Right for more than twenty years." Unlike Anna, Kevin puts himself out there. He attends dance parties and social events and has joined an online gay dating site. When I asked him what he thought the problem was, he replied, "I don't think I am made to have a loving relationship." I thought it was a sad answer, and I said, "Everyone has the birthright to love and be loved. We have to be open to love." Kevin shared his feelings about growing up in a family that argued. "My parents divorced when I was five." I could see that Kevin associated fighting with love and did not have any idea what a true loving relationship looked like. He didn't believe that people were really honest in relationships; he felt that happy couples were putting on *airs*. "It's all a show when they're around people," he said, "but I bet when they're alone, they just argue."

I began to open my mind to see Kevin's point of view. I'll admit that all relationships have their ups and downs, and personalities are apt to clash from time to time, but because we are souls, there is much more to relationships than our human experiences.

We are all part of a soul group, and within the group, we have soul mates—not one, but many. Because we share many lives with our soul group, we accumulate karmic patterns that must be balanced, and we do this best with our soul mates, who are our loving partners in life. Perhaps Kevin's karma began in a previous lifetime when he was a parent to his present-day parents and he behaved harshly toward them. No one is "exempt" from having loving relationships. For Kevin, having a loving relationship may mean that he has to balance his past-life karma by forgiving his parents and be open-minded about the possibility that love can be caring and cooperative.

In contrast, Anna (my cat-loving friend) may have experienced a previous life in which she was abandoned by a love interest. The karmic feelings of that situation may be preventing her from initiating a relationship that might make her vulnerable again. And that's okay. She may need to experience a life in which she steps back from human relationships so that she gains the confidence to accept love into her life. I have learned never to judge how someone leads his or her life. It's all meant to be.

Katie lost Bob, her husband of 22 years, when a drunk driver crashed into his car. As Katie said, "When

Bob died, all the fun died with him." Katie merely "existed," though she was grateful for her two boys. "They're keeping me alive," she said. It was during a conversation with Katie that Bob came through. I told her, "Bob is saying that you will experience love again. He is going to make sure of it." Katie didn't believe it. Her grief was so overwhelming, and she could not accept the vastness that love offers. However, several years later, I was at a gas station when a vehicle drove up beside me. I looked over and saw Katie. She smiled. "How are you?" I asked. "Very well, thank you," she said with a big smile. Then she turned and introduced me to her fiancé, Carl, sitting beside her. It may have taken Katie a while to heal her grief, but with the support of her two boys, she had been able to open her heart and share love once again.

By its very nature, love is sensitive, and either you are ready to open your heart to new situations or you will run and hide. The choice is yours. I believe with each new day there is another opportunity to find love. When you are in a state of loving awareness, you'll be amazed how other people, including strangers, respond to you. Like anything else, the more you practice loving yourself, the more you will become a true love magnet. Everyone will begin to witness your incredible, beautiful energy and want to be a part of it.

Solution: Harmony

To find love in your life, first become aware of the energy around you and the energy you feel when you are with people. You may not see colors or shapes like I do, but you can sense when someone radiates friendly energy and when someone seems closed off. Too many of us are at war with one another. This is an unnatural state of being. If there were no love, only fear would remain, and if there were no fear, only love would remain. The energy of love brings us together and does not separate; it is harmonious. Try as best you can to tune in to the energy of the heart. Feeling balanced and harmonious takes mindful work on your part. No matter how tumultuous the physical dimension seems, practice opening to the higher power of love. Try to put yourself in another person's situation, and perhaps this will foster more compassion and understanding on your part. If you can approach life with a harmonious attitude, you will experience peace, and every person who crosses your path will feel your peace as well.

I am able to feel a loving, balanced
connection with everyone and everything.

How Do I Heal Family Ties?

Although it's not easy to understand, we do choose our parents and siblings and various members of our extended families. They, too, are part of our soul group. We feel a cooperative sense of belonging with such souls. Many of us have had caring parents and siblings, loving aunts and uncles with whom we formed lifelong connections. These connections allow us to expand our love and progress spiritually even more.

However, many people have told me that they would never have chosen a certain parent, brother, aunt, or uncle because their relationship with him or her was terrible. The person was either abusive, domineering, cold, and distant, or lacked any sympathy or understanding. If only we could realize that our families are our greatest teachers because they give us the most opportunities to spiritually grow in forgiveness, harmony, and compassion, then we might not resist the lessons they offer us.

A few years back I read for a woman I will call Liz. Her father had passed away, and she became co-owner of his business with her brother. Her brother, who was older, felt he should run the company his way and didn't want any feedback or advice from Liz. This led to a terrible argument between them, and the two siblings stopped speaking to each other. When her father came through in the reading, he was upset that his children were fighting over a business that he loved and had thought would bring them happiness. I told Liz that her father wanted the two of them to make up so he could rest in peace.

After the reading, I spoke to Liz about blame and resentment. I told her that blaming her brother for her unhappiness was much easier than taking responsibility and changing her thinking. I suggested that she write her brother a letter expressing her feelings, but not send it. "Burn it," I said, "and let the smoke carry your resentment into the atmosphere." I added, "Write a letter to your father and thank him for everything he has given you and your family. He will know what's in your heart." Liz agreed to follow my suggestions, and I could see the colors of her aura begin to change as she opened her heart and mind to the possibility of healing long-held hurt and anger.

Most of the problems within families revolve around personalities and egos, the Earth aspects of our being, not who we are as souls. If we could understand that fear is the motivating factor when someone behaves negatively, then we would have a different reaction. We have to stop the blame game. Every single person on Earth has insecurities and problems. No one can *make you feel anything.* You have to be willing to feel a certain way. Spirit wants us to be happy and joyful. I tell my students that instead of focusing on ill will, *release and just be.* Love cannot enter a judgmental heart. When we recognize our spiritual truth, we are another step closer to connecting to the Oneness.

Solution: Cooperation

Holding grudges and resentment is typical in families. If we can remember that our families are our soul groups, and that we come here to learn together, then there may be less resistance to learning our lessons. A family of souls usually works on a particular theme that could last lifetimes—it could be trust, honesty, ambition, discipline, respect, courage, abundance, and so forth. Souls in a family group have been together in many lifetimes, but not all incarnate at the same time. Sometimes a soul comes in to assist in a particular lesson. Souls decide on which lesson they want to learn, and once all the lessons are learned (this may take hundreds of lifetimes, mind you), the souls decide to part company and move on to form new groups with different souls. Liz and her brother came into life to learn cooperation. When we are able to give and freely work with another person and honor his or her input, opinions, and values, we are living the ideal of cooperation. Many times, two is better than one. If Liz and her brother could cooperate by taking the time to see each other's perspective instead of focusing on having it "my way," then they might create a dynamic business together. Often, the life experiences of someone you trust can prevent you from making similar mistakes. We are here to help each other, so the knowledge you receive is meant to be shared. The power of love is healing, and when shared with another, it becomes transformative.

> I know that every person and experience has
> value for me in fully understanding
> the boundless energy of love.

What Can I Do to Find My Soul Mate?

Because we are all connected, there will be times when you meet someone and you feel an instant bond. Usually, both people are aware of this connection as they search their souls for a feeling or memory involving each other, whether it is a personality trait or common interest, but they know that there was a connection before. And now they meet again because the bonds of love bring us together and those bonds can never be destroyed.

I have met a few people in my life whom I recognize from previous lifetimes. As I shared in *Adventures of the Soul*, Debbie Ford was someone I knew and loved in many lifetimes. When she passed, and appeared to me in Spirit, I was reassured that we would share many more lifetimes with each other. Another soul that touched me was Marilyn Whall. I have been a faculty member of the Omega Institute for 14 years, and during that time I have met hundreds of students from all over the world. But no one has had the effect that Marilyn had. The first time I looked into her eyes and heard her quick, down-to-earth wit, there was no mistaking that she and I had shared many lives, laughs, and loves. Why did we meet again at this particular time? Like me, Marilyn was a medium. And like me, her life was about searching her soul, finding her true path, and eventually sharing stories of the afterlife. No wonder we both chose a time when hearts would be open to hearing our message that *there is no death*.

Several years before I met Marilyn, I was at one of my demonstrations in Ohio. It was a rainy evening, and people were still entering the auditorium as I was speaking. I noticed a male spirit following a young woman to her seat. I remember because her umbrella was dripping water in a line on the floor. Before she could get comfortable, I asked her to stand and say her name. When she did, I told her that her husband wanted to speak to her. He was very concerned about her coming because of the weather. "He is showing me a car accident on a rainy evening just like this one." She nodded. "Why did my husband have to die so young?" was her question to me. Suddenly the Spirit world poured out an answer for the benefit of not only her but the audience as well. "There is no death. Your husband left his body, but his soul is very much alive," I said. "Death is a transformation from one plane of existence to another." I told the young woman that her husband would always be with her. Then he said something that surprised both the audience and me. "Thursday night, you woke up and looked over at the clock on the night table at two sixteen. Is that correct?" Shocked, she responded, "Yes!" I smiled. "He was there." I continued, "The power of love crosses over dimensions. He has been with you in many lifetimes—you are soul mates. He will see you in a future life. You will forever be connected!"

Solution: Elevation

I often find that when we get too emotional, especially when we lose a loved one, we are apt to hold back any good that may be waiting for us. Negative emotions drain our psychological, mental, and physical energy fields. As magnetic beings, the law of attraction draws to us the energy of our thoughts and feelings. In times of emotional stress and strain, if we can elevate our thoughts to something that makes us happy, even for a few minutes, then the energy will help advance us to a new understanding and awareness. Set your intention to raise your awareness and then let it go and let the Universe do its part. A positive action like taking a walk in nature, or puttering around in your garden, or helping a neighbor, will elevate your energy. Any one of these ways makes your heart sing and contributes to enhancing the love inside. When we let go of anxiousness and self-pity, we give the space for love to do its part. It is in giving that we receive, and by spreading cheer and joy in another person's life, we will complain less and laugh more.

> I am ready to use love for the upliftment
> and attunement of my spiritual self.

Understanding the Consequences
of Our Actions

Everyone is a unique self-expression of the Source. This self-expression is an invisible energy vibration that links each one of us to others. So whatever is going on inside of you will extend outward to others.

When I was temping at an employment agency, there was a fellow named Jim whom everyone tried to avoid. I'm sure we've all encountered such a person. His energy was, to say the least, very negative. He never had a nice word for anyone. He complained about the office, the boss, the traffic, the coffee, and so on. When he came into a room, everyone turned away or walked out. I always tried to make a joke to ease the tension in the room, but even I could not overcome Jim's attitude. He was not an easy person to like.

The consequences of Jim's actions made everyone unhappy around him. The more disagreeably he acted, the more unpleasant the results. The bad situations he encountered reinforced his thinking that the world was an unhappy place, so naturally he kept going around and around in a vicious cycle. Jim had no idea that he had the power to change his behavior by raising his awareness. And as everyone knows, once aware, you cannot go back to being unaware.

Years later when I was delving into my psychic studies, I realized that Jim was someone whose energy vibration not only influenced others but also siphoned off the energy of those around him—he was a psychic vampire, if you will. His intensely critical thoughts and feelings were strong enough to create a demoralized atmosphere in the room. It was possible that he was under the influence of negative forces in the forms of guilt, fear, and low self-worth. Like most people, Jim didn't know what kind of energy he was giving out, or getting back, for that matter. However, his pessimistic attitude and insensitivity would eventually catch up with him. Over a prolonged period of time, this type of energy vibration usually drains the body's immune system and can lead to serious illness.

The best way to raise awareness is through meditation, prayer, and practicing forgiveness. For many people, including Jim, sitting in silence for five minutes every day helps to decompress the tension and anxiety of life's responsibilities and burdens. When our minds are calm, our attitudes are more positive, and this good energy permeates the space around us.

MEDITATION—FORGIVENESS

Forgiveness is the very first step on the road to activating the power of love. It is a gift we give ourselves. By forgiving past hurts and releasing expectations, we surrender our souls and begin to activate the greater power of love.

Imagine that you are sitting on a marble bench in a perfectly landscaped garden. This is a magical garden where miracles come true. In your vision, there is an enormous green crystal ball of light that possesses heavenly powers of healing and balance. The energy inside this crystal ball materializes forgiveness and love, and creates clarity from darkness and togetherness from separation. As you take your next breath, place a person in your life whom you need to forgive inside the healing crystal ball. See the person standing there ready to receive your forgiveness and understanding. As you breathe, see the crystal ball of light surrounding the person with forgiveness and love. Then let this person go. Place another person whom you need to forgive inside this ball. Now see that person having a wonderful relationship with you in complete harmony. Then let this person go.

Next, place a situation in your life that needs to be forgiven into the green crystal ball. This can be an event from your past or something that is happening in the present. Let the crystal ball fill the situation with forgiveness and let it go. Finally, place yourself in the middle of the crystal ball so that you can forgive yourself. The most important person to forgive is yourself, so take the time to do it. Be mindful of how you are feeling now that you are finally open to forgiving yourself. See the green light of forgiveness filling you up, then release all pain and punishment you hold against yourself and let it go. Be free.

PART II

PLAYING
THE GAME
OF LIFE

4

EVERYTHING IS ENERGY

"Love is the energy of the soul. Love is what heals the personality. There is nothing that cannot be healed by love. There is nothing but love."

— GARY ZUKAV, *THOUGHTS FROM THE SEAT OF THE SOUL*

Are Thoughts Real Things?

Every day we pass through invisible energy fields composed of thoughts, and if we are sensitive, empathetic, and aware, we can easily be influenced by the energy around us. Everything comes back to its source, and the source is the mind. Our minds hold all the thoughts we have ever had in not only this lifetime but every lifetime. It is the most powerful tool we have—better than any computer. Soul memories build upon soul memories; experiences build upon experiences. Once you have learned a lesson, you can never go backward.

A while back I was on a morning TV show and was asked to read for some of the members in the audience. A determined spirit woman came through and wanted to speak to her daughter. "I have your mother here," I told the daughter. "She said you tried to speak to her." The woman got teary-eyed. "Yes, my mom fell down near her bed," she said. "She yelled my name and I ran into her room. She was already on the floor." I continued, "Your mom wants me to tell you that it's not your fault. You could not have saved her. She says that you run around all the time with the thought *If only I was there five minutes before she fell, I could have saved her!* She doesn't want you to keep doing that. 'Stop that!' she says. 'Stop that!'"

The mother showed me how that negative thought dulled the colors around the head of her daughter. As I continued relaying more of the loving message from her mom, I could see the dullness fading away and being replaced by a bright purplish-pink. I could tell that this mother's message assisted her daughter in realizing that the constant rehashing of the same thought over and over in her mind affected not only herself but also her mother in Spirit. Thoughts are a two-way street even across dimensions. No one who loves us wants to see us in unnecessary pain.

Like this woman, many of us beat ourselves up over and over again about how we should've or could've done something in a situation that is long gone and truly out of our control. A spirit once told an audience member, "I died once. Don't make me die every day with your thoughts!" Because our thoughts and feelings are magnetic, they are conductors of our physical and mental health. Every cell of our body is directed to do its job by the subconscious part of our mind. When we persist in having negative thoughts of worry, remorse, regret, guilt, and the like, we are passing on these suggestions to our subconscious minds. We literally attack ourselves in our minds. Over time, the subconscious will act upon these thoughts by making the body sick. As the mother said to the daughter, *Stop that!*

Solution: Causality

For every action, there is a reaction. That is the nature of the law of cause and effect. A thought is made up of energy, color, denseness, and design, and it is propelled by your intention. We are the result of our thoughts. If your thoughts are continually filled with guilt and fear, the results will show up in your life as negative behaviors and situations. Ask yourself about the recent events in your life. What was good? What was negative? What did you say? What did the other person say? Assess your answers. Be honest. Then ask yourself, "What energy am I holding on to right now in my belief systems, behavior patterns, feelings, and relationships that is not serving my highest good?" Spend a few moments and see what comes to mind. All cause begins in your mind. If you can release something from the past, such as any sadness or guilt trip, even for a few moments, you are healing yourself. If you desire a life filled with love, you must raise your thoughts to be more loving. By accelerating the energy of love, you will attract more joy, happiness, and abundance into your future.

I am fully aware that the amount of love I create in my thoughts is a powerful foundation for the results I want.

Creating a New Mind-Set

Because thoughts are energy, an accumulation of thoughts becomes a belief system, or mind-set. A positive mind-set raises your soul vibration and a negative mind-set lowers it. Souls whose energies are in the low echelons of thought gravitate to concepts and individuals that are like-minded. The same is true of souls with higher energies—they gravitate to ideas and people on the same wavelength. We have the power to change our soul vibration by elevating our thoughts and beliefs, and, in turn, inspiring others to illuminate their souls' energies.

Many of us send mixed messages to the Universe —that we want something but in our hearts we feel undeserving, or that it doesn't matter because we never get what we want anyway. Beliefs that begin in childhood based on the words of our parents are often born of the signs of the time, and many of us still hold on to outdated beliefs. If you were taught to fear the unknown, you may feel isolated and separated in unfamiliar surroundings. That was how I felt as a young boy.

As a child, I could not explain the ghostly things I heard and felt that no one else could. I felt different and set apart from other children. I might have grown to be a very fearful person. Fortunately, I had a mother who was wise enough to support me and protect me from other people's condemnation. Our beliefs and mind-set are products of our environment, but we can transform even the most deep-rooted beliefs. All thoughts and beliefs form what we experience. When a particular behavior is repeated often enough, it molds a "new" you. Meditation actually can change the way we think and react to life's situations. Scientific studies have shown that meditation develops the neocortex of the brain, which in turn enhances our ability to learn.

If we are willing to open to the possibility that there is more to life than what we know with our physical senses, then we will be closer to understanding the perfection of our souls. Dedicate yourself to a belief system that embraces trust, respect, and love, and the boundaries between you and others will begin to fade.

How Can I Lessen My Fears and Negativity?

Your thoughts not only affect your body but also influence the invisible energy field that encircles you—your aura. An aura appears like a glass shell or envelope around the physical body. Before I begin a demonstration, I scan the auras surrounding people in the audience. I can see colors, light, dark, holes, tears, leaks, and an assortment of psychic phenomena. I am made aware of overindulgent behaviors, like addiction to cigarettes, alcohol, drugs, caffeine, and food, because anything in excess causes energetic loss in the aura. Emotional hurts, heartaches, and upsets show up in people's auras. These behaviors not only cause stress in the physical dimension but also can cause harm from dimensions of which we are not aware.

I was at a Whole Life Expo several years ago when the spirit of a young woman appeared to her mother, who was in the audience. I had a woozy feeling in my head and asked the mother if her daughter had passed from an overdose of drugs. The mother nodded yes. As the daughter began to project her image at the time of her passing into my mind, I could see that her aura was dark and muddy, and there seemed to be two entities hovering around her. According to her mother, the young woman had hung out with a dangerous drug crowd. "Your daughter opened her energy field to unwanted psychic attack," I said. Explaining further, I told the woman that her daughter had been manipulated by her own fears.

Although the mother had tried to get her daughter into rehab, it was impossible because the daughter was susceptible to direction by these lower-level addictive forces. The more drugs she took, the more open she was to being manipulated and influenced. I tried to explain what I was seeing as best I could without scaring the rest of the audience. The mother explained that one young man in particular had been controlling her daughter. After her daughter's death, a detective had told her that this fellow had been arrested and sent to jail for drug dealing. I explained that her daughter was safe on the other side and that the love of the spirit world had assisted her in cleaning up her mind and her addictive behavior. "There is an aunt there helping your daughter to recuperate." The mother was relieved. "Thank God for my sister," she replied. The young woman told her mother that she was sorry for the pain she had caused and repeated "I love you" over and over.

Behavior that is out of control or too extreme is always based on thoughts of fear. Fear has a way of twisting all our thoughts and feelings, causing us to become destructive to ourselves and others. Because of my ability to see auras and sense the energetic world of spirits, I have come across some spirits that have caused disturbance to the living by entering their auric fields and influencing their souls. Constant fear, including feelings of doom and gloom, distrust, and hopelessness, is an open invitation to negative astral entities. You have to be aware that there is a world beyond the three-dimensional physical universe. Pay attention to your feelings, especially when you are around other people and places. If something doesn't feel "right" to you, it is probably a signal from your inner self that you should be alert to your surroundings.

When we abuse our bodies and minds, we impair our auric fields, and it becomes easy for others to take advantage of us. Our goal is to release fear and love ourselves, because no one can make us do anything unless we allow them to.

Solution: Release

It is important to be aware that you are an energetic being, not just a body. Because people constantly send out thoughts, you are literally walking through a minefield of energy every day, and you must be conscious of where you step. You have no control over the intentions behind the energies of others, but you *can* control your own thoughts. You have the power to release the stagnant energy of old behaviors. If you are sensitive, you are probably very aware of the foreign energies surrounding you and therefore do not walk into them. In the case of the young woman above, she had so little love for herself that she became a victim with no power to determine her own destiny. She was mentally weak from an inferior self-image. She thought of herself as unattractive and undesirable, and therefore was easily manipulated. Doing drugs opened holes in her aura that allowed the lower fear energies of those around her to influence her behavior. We all have the ability to free unwanted energy by releasing our fears and negativity to the loving force of the Universe.

> I have the ability to free unwanted energy
> to the loving force of the Universe.

Aligning Your Energy

Having a strong and healthy aura can be life-saving. Our auras have many layers, and each layer coincides with the physical, emotional, mental, and spiritual aspects of our souls. Any excessive negative thinking, worry, or tension can cause leaks, tears, and other defects in one or more layers of your aura. Over time, you can feel exhausted and overwhelmed. In order to keep ourselves well and balanced, we must release any stagnant energy of addictive and destructive behaviors. Accept your fears and then gently let them go; don't give them any unnecessary power.

Get into a ritual every day to align your energy. Make an attempt to sit in the stillness of your being—even if it is only for five minutes. Imagine a green light emanating from your beautiful heart and let this loving green light surround the entire atmosphere around you. Be mindful that Mother Earth is like a magnet, and she will pull energies from your auric field that are not in harmony with your soul being. As you visualize this, the power of love for yourself increases. You will notice a difference immediately. The more love you feel, the more energies that are detrimental to your spiritual health will be released.

Another great technique is to clear your aura in the shower. As the spray of water flows over the top of your head, imagine any foreign, negative, or stagnant energy that you may have been holding on to washing away. See it flowing from the tips of your fingers and toes and down the drain. Once all the unwanted energy floats away, imagine your aura beginning to fill with a golden light, creating new, vibrant energy. When you make the effort to remove any negativity from your atmosphere, you make room for the positive to replace it.

MEDITATION—CAUSALITY

In your mind's eye, visualize two giant screens side by side. On the left screen is a timeline of your life arranged in years and decades. Choose a year or decade to observe. Very quickly, a few significant situations will begin to stand out. See them, live them, and be them. As you do this, you will find that there are one or two particular events that are emotionally prominent. With an objective eye, immerse yourself in the particular circumstances surrounding the event and become aware of the various choices and decisions you made at that time.

Now, turn to the right screen and observe the outcomes resulting from the choices you made—for not only the other recipients but yourself as well. Clearly see the energy you created with your actions and the rippling effect caused by your words and deeds. As these memories and events come into clarity, begin to see the sources of and reasons for the decisions that you made. Become completely aware of the motives, insights, and reasoning that were involved. While doing this, it is important to be as objective as possible, remembering that you are now at a very different place and time in your life. You also might find that nothing has changed very significantly in your decision-making process and you might make the same choices again, given the same circumstances.

Imagine the light of love entering both screens until they are both clear. Realize that the power of love can expand your life choices and extend to all those within your sphere. All choices are based on either fear or love. Become more aware than ever of which one has been the most frequent cause of your decisions. See how it has shaped the life you now live. From this moment on, you know you want a life full of love, so begin to choose love as the cause of your choices. As you express love in all you do and are, you will see its ripples expanding beyond your everyday existence.

5

MAKING DECISIONS

*"Every person, all the events of your life
are there because you have drawn them there.
What you choose to do with them is up to you."*

— RICHARD BACH, *ILLUSIONS*

Choices and Destiny

I believe that when it comes to making choices, many of us sit on the fence because we are afraid to make the wrong one. Life is made up of choices; it is a series of decisions, and any one decision can change our lives. What is important to you? What you value may not be as important to someone else. When you feel anxious and confused about a particular life decision, take the time to meditate and ask Spirit for help. The answer may not come right away, but if you are consistent in your meditation, Spirit will often guide you. It may not be what you expected, but it will be the right choice for your soul's evolvement.

Some choices may be simply a matter of preference, like my friend Max's. Max and I were sitting at an outdoor café one day when a black BMW sedan cruised by us. Max commented, "That's such a great-looking car. I've always liked that model." I asked, "Why don't you get one, if you like it so much?" I knew Max could afford to drive pretty much any car he wanted. He explained that he and his son were huge baseball fans. "We love to watch the Anaheim Angels play." Besides cheering for their team at the home stadium, Max and his son would travel to different cities a couple of times a year to watch the Angels on the road. "Not having a big car payment gives me the spare cash to support our passion for baseball guilt-free, and I wouldn't trade the experiences we've had for anything!" Max had made a conscious choice regarding where to spend his money and his energy.

On the other hand, there are choices where we don't have control over the outcome; however, we do have control over how we react to the outcome. These are the life-changing decisions. I am a firm believer that souls have various destiny points that we must live through in our lifetimes. These destiny points have been implanted in each soul's makeup before incarnating into the physical world. Yes, we have predetermined paths, but with free will there is always the possibility that we will change our minds and take another path.

When we are "in between" lifetimes in the Spirit world, we will sit with our guides and teachers to carefully evaluate and plan our upcoming life's lessons. We will decide which experiences are necessary to balance karmic obligations and advance our spiritual evolution. These experiences are our destiny points. Many of these destiny points will involve other souls, usually family members or friends in our soul group. The moment a soul actually takes its first breath at birth, all plans made in Spirit are brought forth and put into motion. However, we still have free will and can choose not to fulfill a particular destiny point. For example, destiny may dictate that you meet a particular person and have a relationship to balance out past karma, but at that specific moment when you meet, you decide not to get involved. There are many factors that can influence your free will—the person's appearance, socioeconomic background, the environment, etc. You will have a chance to meet again and balance the karma in another lifetime.

A soul that honestly wants to advance must take the time to go within and contemplate. Only through meditation and prayer will you intuitively know which decisions are destiny points, and only then can you hear the authenticity of your soul's voice and know the correct choice to make. One could say that these destiny points urge a soul to reincarnate. Your destiny is always chosen by your soul, and when you live in accordance with your soul's mission, you move more quickly along the spiritual highway.

As a soul, it is your responsibility to create thought patterns that encompass the highest aspects of compassion and benevolence, not only toward others but also toward yourself. I often say, "Take the HIGH road less traveled." Always remember, what you give out, you will get back. That is a basic rule of the Universe. Give to others what you want to receive. Before you judge another, realize that you have no idea what someone else's motivation may be. Responsible people live by example and teach others through inspiration. People feel your energy, and the more loving your energy is, the more people will be attracted to you. I will often say to my audiences that the hardest part of my work is communicating not with the Spirit world, but with the human world.

How Can I Turn Failure into Success?

I once had a friend, Denise, who was going through a tough period. She was a single mother raising a 12-year-old daughter. She left a well-paying job to start her own business. It was a risk, but she felt in her heart that it was "now or never." For two years she struggled to make a go of her business, but her money ran out and she had to find a job. She sent out her résumé and went on interviews, but being out of work for two years was an obstacle. Denise felt like a failure and thought she had made the biggest mistake of her life by leaving a good job.

While Denise was stressing out, a friend asked Denise to join her on a weekend retreat. "I can't go on a retreat," she said. "I have to find a job." But her friend insisted that the experience would help her, and Denise reluctantly agreed to go. It was a silent retreat in the mountains, and Denise spent time meditating with the group and walking the trails and breathing in the crisp, cool air. For the first time in a long while, Denise began to relax and tune in to herself. When she returned home, I could see in her eyes that she was more peaceful. I asked her what had happened on the retreat. "James," she said with a smile, "I had a vision that was so vivid and real—I saw a train filled with people. But this was no ordinary train; it was a train of light. I could see people, but they were not really bodies—they were light. I knew that I was on the train and at the same time watching the train. I felt so happy. It's hard to describe how great I felt. I knew that I was going to be okay. You know, James, I think I saw a glimpse of eternity, and it was pure, never-ending love." Soon after her insight, Denise got a job developing a business plan for an environmentally conscious start-up company.

Solution: Detachment

Denise faced a destiny point when she decided to go out on her own. Unfortunately, she relied more on her ego than her spiritual self to guide her. When she went off on a retreat (another destiny point), she experienced her soul's voice and was able to release her feelings of failure and relinquish control of knowing how to "fix" her situation. Through meditation and self-awareness, she found the light within herself. Going out on her own wasn't a mistake because it led her to her true path. In the end, her real destiny was to work with other like-minded individuals at a start-up company that was destined to impact many people for the good.

When we detach from our ego's insistent thoughts of lack, failure, and negativity, we can more easily come to our spiritual center to create a sense of calm and stillness. It is not giving up; it is giving in to a state of balance and peace. When we surrender the ego's fear and judgment and become neutral, the space is open for love to enter. Denise realized that she wasn't alone, she was connected to a Source—in her mind a train—of pure light and love. Remember, dear soul, we are merely passing through, and as the Native Americans believe, we don't own anything; we are caretakers for the short time that we are here.

> I am releasing old patterns, ideas, and belief systems that no longer serve the highest ideals of love and evolvement.

What Can I Do about Unrealistic Expectations?

The Universe tests us all on a daily basis. Our job is to maintain balance through the good and bad times, and as we know, there will always be good and bad times. If we have unrealistic expectations or think that everything will stay the same, when something does change, it will be a rude awakening. For example, no one would have imagined that we would be facing yet another recession when the economy went into a nosedive almost a decade ago.

My friend's cousin, Ray, had a beautiful home, a boat, and a cabin on the lake. He had never expected to lose his job during the economic downturn. Ray worked in Detroit and had a wife, three children, and a mortgage. He worked for a company that did all of its business with the car manufacturers. When the car companies needed a bailout from the government, Ray's company was in trouble too, and it began to lay off its workers. Ray was laid off with the promise that as soon as things got better, he would be called back to work. No one foresaw the depth of the recession, and at the beginning, Ray felt sure he would be hired back within a few months. His wife had a part-time job at the local grocery chain, but her salary wasn't enough to pay the bills, and the family's savings were quickly shrinking. Ray realized that things wouldn't improve as quickly as he'd thought, so he put his properties up for sale. But no one was buying anything. He frantically sent out résumés. He went on several interviews, but was never called back. At one point, he was posting three hundred résumés a week on the Internet. He thought that surely he could get a job with his two master's degrees and 15 years' experience in his field.

Finally, Ray's old company called him back. The company had gone into receivership and regrouped. Ray felt all his troubles were finally over when he was offered a job. But when he was given the details—that he would be in a lower-level position with half the salary—Ray declined the offer. Even though half of something was better than nothing, Ray felt humiliated, angry, and defeated. He'd expected to be treated better than he was. He took out his frustrations on his family. He became irritated with his children and argued with his wife. He blamed his old company for causing his troubles. In the end, Ray found a new job, but there was a lot of heartache that had to be healed.

Solution: Ownership

If you are in a crisis like Ray, don't place unneeded worry where it doesn't belong. It is wasted energy. Recognize that life is ever-changing and nothing stays the same. Stay focused on what you can do so you can view your experiences objectively. Blaming others is not the answer. By taking ownership of your choices, you allow each day to bring new insights about the next steps that are available to you. Don't look back at situations and see them as failures; instead, view them as valuable feedback that will help you to learn and grow. When you take ownership of your thoughts, words, and actions, there is a true shift in behavior. Difficult situations like losing a job become opportunities for you to put the power of love into place. In tough situations, remind yourself that you are a soul and you have many opportunities to shine your light and illuminate your space. This will project your confidence to others.

I take possession of all my misdeeds as well as my accomplishments and love them all as lessons.

What Is Real Security?

As Ray found out the hard way, being secure is not about how much money we have or how many possessions we own. It is about remembering that we are spiritual beings. At one of my workshops, I met Bill, a man in his mid 50s who seemed to have an incredible gift of insight, healing, and mediumship. But Bill was afraid to explore his abilities. Throughout the week, we did many exercises in self-empowerment and opening up to our souls' work. I noticed that Bill understood many of the things I was speaking about but had a hard time incorporating them into his world. It wasn't until I lectured, *"What other people think of you is none of your business,"* that I saw Bill break down and cry. He said, "I think I am possessed and an instrument of the devil because I see dead people and can heal the sick." Immediately, I realized that seeing spirits was against his belief system. The work we had been doing had brought his fear and guilt to the surface to be healed.

Bill explained that he was a Catholic priest. "I had nowhere to go but to your workshop. I knew you had your own history of attending seminary school." (In my first book, *Talking to Heaven*, I described my early Catholic upbringing and my enrollment in seminary school to prepare to become a priest. My being a priest was actually my mother's dream, not mine. After one year of seminary teachings, I knew that the God of the Bible was not the God I kept in my heart—the Oneness of unlimited love, compassion, and acceptance.)

I told Bill that all of us bring a history of prior lives and experiences, and no matter what we learn in this life, if it does not apply to our prior knowledge, it will not work for us now. "Your truth is your truth," I explained. Bill felt that the dogma of the church went against everything that Christ stood for in his heart. I told him that evil is a concept of man that is intended to produce fear and allow control over others, and he agreed. Bill then said something quite profound. "It has taken me fifty-four years to finally see the truth— the church is man-made, but God is spirit-made." Everyone in the class stood up and applauded.

You must do what is in your heart. No one can give you your own truth but yourself. Because of this priest's breakthroughs, several other students came forward and acknowledged their powers.

Solution: Freedom

Our natural state is one of boundless freedom and joy, and you must not suppress your God-given potential by weighing yourself down with other people's opinions. Sometimes we present a false facade to feel accepted or included. My Catholic priest friend spent an entire lifetime in a conflict between what he felt inside and the teachings of the church. He was certainly doing a disservice to his soul's mission, the church, and all the people who relied on him for support and comfort. Self-reflection and contemplation, and perhaps a workshop or support group, can help you see a different perspective. Once you release self-imposed restrictions and perceived limitations and are open and honest with yourself, you will have an incredible feeling of empowerment and freedom.

I have released any self-imposed restrictions or perceived limitations through the loving energy of openness.

How Do I Walk My Talk?

Several years ago I wrote a book entitled *Growing Up in Heaven* about the grief over the death of a child. I hadn't planned to write such a book until I began seeing spirit children running around in my office. My spirit guides told me that these children were going to help me write a book to help parents. Over the years I had received hundreds of heartbreaking and heartwarming letters from parents sharing their stories, and I had kept them filed away. These letters formed the basis of the book. Losing a child can be the most difficult challenge for anyone to face, but I do believe that no matter how agonizing the pain, even the death of a child is a lesson. We think of children as innocent, but everyone is a soul, and every soul has experienced many lifetimes. These lives become the blueprint for the soul's spiritual evolution. So when a child dies, it isn't a "child," but a soul—sometimes a very old soul—and there is definitely a purpose for his or her short life on Earth.

When I do readings for parents who have lost a child, I am respectful of their beliefs. It's not my job to impose my beliefs on them, because I know that not everyone believes as I do. Everyone is on a different path, and I honor that. I don't expect to convert everyone to my beliefs, but as a spiritual teacher, and to be true to myself, I share my beliefs with others. When I bring through evidential information for someone in a demonstration or workshop, I also bring through the spiritual lesson associated with the information. The lesson is not only for my audience but also for me, and like them, I take it all in.

Years ago, I was in Indio, California, doing a demonstration in front of a capacity audience of 1,100 people. I never know what's going to happen when I open to Spirit, so I am always just as surprised as everyone else. The readings were coming to an end when a young female spirit came through. I immediately sensed a choking sensation and put my hands up to my neck. As I described what I was seeing and feeling, a woman in the audience raised her hand. The spirit showed me an image of her death—she was hanging from a tree. "That sounds like Carol, my daughter," the woman said.

"What is your name?" I asked. "Francie," she replied. "Carol is sorry to cause you so much pain," I told her. Francie was very understanding. She related, "Carol was pregnant and didn't want the baby. The boy she was dating injected her with some kind of speed, and she went out and hung herself." There was an audible gasp from the audience. I thought, *Oh my God, this poor woman.* Francie did not seem as fazed as the rest of us. At the end of the reading, I said to her, "Please come and see me afterward."

Later, Francie joined the backstage crowd, and when she reached me, I thanked her for coming and sharing her story. She said, "I wanted to ask you about my son." I looked at her. "Your son?" "Yes," she said, "he killed himself, too." She said this with such peacefulness that I was taken aback. Francie confided that both of her children had been overweight and ridiculed at school and on social media. Instead of wallowing in grief, Francie had taken it upon herself to become an advocate for stopping childhood bullying as her coping mechanism. She told me that she visited high schools and shared her story in large auditoriums full of teenagers. As she was telling me this, I was instantly able to make contact with her son, who mentioned that he had helped his sister come through during the reading. He told his mother that she is doing the work of God and that it had to happen this way in order for others to hear her story. I told Francie, "He is saying you are a healing force." Her eyes started to mist and I couldn't help but think of the phenomenal way that Francie had turned what was obviously a horrendous Earth lesson into a positive for herself and others. This courageous woman was a very advanced soul, and all whose presence she graced felt her healing touch upon their souls.

Solution: Integrity

So many of us on our spiritual journeys read many books about spirituality and go to lectures and workshops to improve ourselves, and yet we still criticize ourselves and others. Sometimes we judge others for not doing things the way we are doing them. We think they're not "getting it" the way they should. So many spiritual seekers talk about love, but treat people badly. There is a great chasm between believing in love and compassion and demonstrating these qualities to the world. It could have been quite easy for the mother of two suicides to live with resentment, guilt, and blame, but she chose to see her experience with the passing of her children as a way to help others facing the same struggle they had had. She not only expressed integrity in her beliefs but also showed humility in the face of tragedy. We must remember that every fault we see in others is an aspect of ourselves that we have to try to understand or forgive. To have integrity, you must understand what is meaningful to you and be courageous enough to make choices based upon that knowledge. When you have integrity, you walk the talk of your beliefs.

> I demonstrate the truth and honesty of my
> soul and manifest love in all that I do.

MEDITATION—OWNERSHIP

Imagine that you are standing in a large room. Above the door is a sign reading INSIGHTS. As you peruse the room, you can see many different types of ornate windows. Some windows are highly adorned, multipaned, Victorian in style, while others are clear and modern looking, and still others are tinted, or perhaps stained glass. Some are circular, while others are square or rectangular. The windows do have one thing in common: each has a curtain drawn across it.

As you glance around the room, you find that you gravitate toward specific windows. You move to one window at a time, and as you look at the curtain on the window, a word appears on the fabric. These words represent your life lessons. For instance, you may see EMPATHY, JUDGMENT, FRIENDSHIP, HONESTY, TRUST, ENVY, etc. After the word appears, the curtain opens and you look through the window. What immediately comes into view is a vision of a life situation in which you learned or attempted to learn that particular lesson. As you see the images, try to identify within the situation when you were using love and when you were not. Without judging yourself, evaluate how much easier things would have been if you had gone deep within your soul self and utilized the great force of love.

After you have looked through as many windows as you can, leave the room. Look up at the sign above the door and realize that you have gained invaluable insight into your spiritual journey.

PART III

ACCEPTANCE

6

SURRENDERING

*"Let us always meet each other with a smile,
for the smile is the beginning of love."*

— MOTHER TERESA

How Can I Surrender to the
Oneness of Love?

I usually meet people when they are still filled with grief over their loss of a loved one, and it's difficult to tell these people to be grateful for the time they shared with the person. It takes time to mourn a loved one, and everyone grieves differently. Grieving and healing are parts of a process. We may not understand the process of transitioning from this life to the next, but it suffices to say that our loved ones are no longer limited by a human body. Once we realize that there is no such thing as death, and that our loved ones are always around us, healing can begin.

In 2014, I did the *Radio Caravan* show in Southern California. The show's co-host, Robert Palmer, had just passed away. Months before he passed, I had been scheduled to be a guest, but the schedule was changed, so instead I arrived at the radio station just after his passing. When I arrived, I said to the host, Scott Hays, "Spirit rearranges things for everyone's benefit." Robert's wife and daughter were there at the studio, and I had the opportunity to bring in Robert. "Robert is honored to be here," I said quickly. "He is talking about a big memorial service and another smaller one. He's talking about going to the beach in Hawaii." I explained that I felt something in my throat, that Robert's death was sudden, and that he couldn't speak before passing over. "He's very adventurous, likes to travel and do different things. He's laughing. He's okay. 'I'm alive,' he says."

As I tuned in to Robert's energy, I could tell there was something special about him. He was a very spiritual guy—not religious in the conventional way. "Robert is a cool guy," I continued. "He doesn't want you to be sad." I asked his wife, Nancy, if she was thinking of having another service for him. "He wants a party—he wants everyone to lighten up. Don't take yourselves too seriously." As I shared the communication, I could tell that Robert had lived his life to the fullest and that he was always searching for the next adventure. At the end of the program, I could tell that everyone's energy had lightened up, and they thanked me for being there at the right time. I have no doubt that Spirit orchestrated the scheduling conflict so that Robert's family could receive that healing. What at first blush seemed to me to be an annoying problem with logistics turned out to provide the best possible resolution for all concerned. It was my fault for not surrendering and understanding that all things happen in divine order.

Solution: Gratitude

People are always thanking me for bringing through their loved ones, and I am also grateful for the work that I do. As we consciously experience gratitude, we are mindful that even the simplest parts of our lives are wondrous and miraculous. When we stop focusing on what we don't have and instead appreciate what we do have, we immediately feel more content and happier "in the moment." Every moment seems more precious. Granted, heartbreaking things happen in this physical dimension, but if we can acknowledge that there is a Source with a divine plan and accept that we are part of this plan, we will be able to look at misfortune—even the death of a loved one—as a gift. A thankful heart is limitless.

At the end of each day when you get into bed, say a prayer of gratitude and send it out to everyone around the world, and especially to those who taught you that day, whether through upset, hurt, love, or laughter. Good things come from practicing gratitude. I've seen over and over how giving thanks makes people happier, improves their relationships with others, and even enhances their physical and mental health.

> I fully appreciate the invaluable
> and loving lessons that life presents.

How Can I Have a More Loving Perspective?

As you get a sense of love for yourself, you will begin to see the light in every person. Instead of quickly judging someone, take a moment to pause and see the person in that light. Be open to the new and different and allow love to be the norm.

My father was very skeptical of my work. He would watch me on TV and was proud of me, but he really didn't believe in an afterlife. I certainly thought that after seeing me do it so many times, he would be convinced that I was communicating with the Spirit world, but he never was. We all want approval, especially from our parents, but I could not live my truth based on my father's beliefs, and vice versa. When he passed over, I felt his spirit presence almost immediately.

Usually spirits need time to adjust to their new environment, but my father came to me moments after his passing and said very clearly, "Oh, Jamie, you got it right! I'm alive! I've seen your mother. I met a sister I didn't know." (His mother had miscarried.) After that, my father frequently came to me, and I began writing down everything he told me about the conditions and atmosphere around him. He described how beautiful things were in heaven compared to on Earth. He remarked, "The Earth is like quicksand, and we are happy to be free of the quicksand." Spirits have often told me that the energy of the Earth plane is heavy and dense. I have a file full of information that my father gave me from the other side. It amuses me because he was such a skeptic as a human, but as a spirit he is so like a butterfly that has emerged from its cocoon.

My father had to wait until he crossed over to become aware of his spiritual self. He was closed off to this kind of information, and that was okay, for it was his soul's journey. I could have gotten frustrated with him, but I knew that I made a difference in his life, as he had in mine. Nothing could be more satisfying.

Solution: Respect

It is important to respect everyone's journey in this physical dimension. As spiritual beings, we all struggle with the human obstacles that are our individual lessons. It wasn't my job to judge my father for not seeing life the way I do. He had chosen his life blueprint, just as I chose mine. By showing my respect, I earned his. When you value everyone's unique perspective on his or her individual path to love, you are showing respect. One of my favorite books is *To Kill a Mockingbird* by Harper Lee. I will never forget the line Atticus Finch says to his daughter, Scout: *"You never really know a man until you stand in his shoes and walk around in them."* When you respect another, you are allowing yourself to see the bigger picture, past the illusion of race, gender, religious beliefs, or social status. You accept others as equals because we are all part of the picture simply trying to show each other the way to go home.

I value each person's unique
perspective on his or her path to love.

Creating Balance in Your Life

I was in New Jersey doing an evening presentation to a crowd of 700 people. One of the most profound messages of the evening came from a spirit named Joe, who wanted to tell his wife that he was fine and that she needed to get back into life. "You have to treat life as a gift," he told her. Suzanne, his wife, had given up since Joe had passed on. She spent most of her days in front of the TV. He wanted her to know that he was always watching over her and that she had to start living again. Suzanne heard the message loud and clear and began to cry her eyes out. I asked her, "How long has it been since Joe passed?" She blurted, "Forty-two years!" Suzanne was holding on to the memory of her husband for far too long. In order to bring balance back into her life, she had to surrender the loss of her loved one. Once she realized that, she had no more excuses to procrastinate and had to get on with living her life.

A few years ago I did a reading for a man in an audience who had lost his mother and brother. Dan was very emotional as he spoke. "I feel my mother very strongly; she is around me every day. But I haven't felt my brother's presence." He told me that his brother had passed two months earlier. I explained that there is an adjustment period when spirits reach the other plane. When a person lingers with an illness, it takes time to adjust to a whole new way of life on the spirit side. They have to build up their pranic energy—their vitality—before they're ready to communicate. It takes a lot of energy for a spirit to manipulate its vibration so it can put its thoughts into our minds.

In this instance, Dan was in such a state of anxiety over trying to hear from his brother in Spirit that he delayed receiving any communication. I told him, "Relax, your brother is already around you. You just can't hear him because you are blocked. Calm yourself and listen. You will feel he's around when you clear your mind."

We all have busy schedules, and most of us are guilty of being out of balance. We put too much emphasis on one part of our lives and too little on another. This is not healthy. Suzanne lived in the past and Dan lived in the future. Neither of them had a balanced outlook on life. The best ways to balance yourself when you feel anxious, unhappy, and overwhelmed is to take a moment to breathe. Quiet your mind and live in the present. Practicing the meditations at the end of every chapter in this book will help you create more balance and healing in your life.

How Can I Be More Receptive to My Soul Self?

Just consider that most of the energy of your soul resides outside the body, and only about 20 percent resides in the body. If we could see energy, we would barely be able to delineate the point where our own soul energy ends and the universal energy begins. There is no separation. The Spirit world often refers to this joined energy as "stardust." As human beings, we are aware of the world through the physical sensor of the brain. Another word for this awareness is *consciousness*. There is also an unconscious, involuntary level of our human makeup that keeps the body doing things like breathing and circulating blood. But there are levels of consciousness beyond the human spectrum in which you are in constant contact with *everything*. But your conscious awareness is shielded from this because the human brain is not able to process that information.

The energy of the soul is not limited to its physical, human aspect, but the laws of the physical three-dimensional world do not apply in other dimensions. To measure a soul would be similar to measuring a thought. The Spirit world has often communicated to me that humans cannot even come close to comprehending the enormity of the soul. It would be like saying the toe is the whole body. The body is the tip of the iceberg. The essence of our soul's energy resides beyond the human body and beyond the aura in the vastness of limitless Oneness.

So, opening yourself to the world around you should not be as difficult as you may think. Get out of the "Earth mind" and into the "Spirit mind." Because spirits communicate through fast-moving thought, I have to raise my vibration to feel spirits that live at a higher level. Thirty years of meditation have enabled me to connect with them at that level.

Before one of my demonstrations, I was backstage sitting in a dressing room when a spirit came to me. He was anxious to communicate with his brother, who was in the audience. Usually before I begin my demonstrations, I clear my mind of anything that might be happening and sit in silence to raise my inner power. But this particular spirit kept interrupting my meditation until I agreed to go to his brother first.

When I stepped onstage, I saw the same spirit standing behind a middle-aged man with his arms crossed over his chest. I knew this man did not want to be there. His wife or friend had probably brought him, kicking and screaming all the way. I could tell that he did not want to be involved in anything that was taking place. I pointed to him. "May I speak to you?" He looked at me and then turned around to see if I was talking to the person behind him. "No, I mean you! Your brother is here and is very anxious to speak with you. Can you stand, please, and tell me your name?" The woman next to him pushed him to stand up, and reluctantly he got to his feet. "Smith," he said. "Your first name," I said, smiling. "Jerry Smith," he grumbled. "I gotta say, your brother is very insistent. He came to me backstage and wants to talk to you. Do you understand?" The man nodded ever so slightly. "He is telling me about a car—an old car. I see him fixing a car. Does this make sense?" The man's eyes lit up. "Yes." I let out a sigh of relief. "Thank God! I have to tell you that he wants you to know that you have to do something with this car. Don't give up, he says. Don't give up. Do you understand?" At this moment, the man let out his first sign of emotion. "Yeah. Tell

Ben I understand." The woman next to him put her hand on his back. "Your brother loves you a lot," I said. "He did a lot to get here. He is a persistent guy. He is saying that he will be with you and the car. He is very happy to be here with you. He loves you, bro, he says. Oh, he is also showing me the odometer. One hundred and twenty-two thousand miles!"

At the end of the demonstration, Jerry Smith came up to me. I could tell that he'd been crying. "I didn't want to come, but my wife dragged me here." I nodded in understanding. "My brother, Ben, and I had a dream of restoring classic cars. He loved the big cars of the '50s. When he died, I just covered up the old Mercury. I couldn't figure anything out anymore. I felt lost without his help."

I smiled at Jerry and said, "I know it is hard right now, but your brother wants you to continue. He hangs around you. I kept seeing this blue car with the hood raised, but I didn't understand. Now it makes sense. I guess you've got some work to do." Jerry answered with a smile, "You bet I do. Oh, and by the way, it's true—that Mercury has 122,000 miles on it. He was right!" I replied, "He just wants to prove to you that you have not lost him. He will always help you!" Once Jerry was receptive to the love of his brother from the Spirit world, he was able to release his grief and self-doubt, and his passion for restoring old cars was renewed.

Solution: Creativity

One of the natural characteristics of the soul is creation. Spirit constantly inspires our souls to express who we are. In this case, Jerry was being inspired by his brother in Spirit to continue with the creative work they had done together to restore old cars. Jerry had been so closed off to his soul self that he was unable to access the love of his brother. The more Jerry wallowed in grief and sadness, the bigger the wall he built around himself became. The wall kept any creativity from flowing into him. When we block our creativity through bitterness, isolation, and hopelessness, we cannot fully live the expression of our souls. We all recognize that creative people are tuned in to something beyond themselves. A creative person often receives new ideas, solutions, and possibilities through intuition and inspiration. The more we allow ourselves to be instruments of love, the more we can tune in to the higher creative energy and bring heaven onto Earth.

> I am attuned to my soul energy and devise
> new ideas, concepts, and forms of illumination.

MEDITATION—RESPECT

Imagine that you are sitting on a moving train filled with passengers. As you look around, you see a complete mixture of people—men and women, young and old, from different socioeconomic and cultural backgrounds. Some are well dressed, others are casual, and some don't seem to care what they wear. Some are lost in reading or listening to music, while others are daydreaming and looking out the window.

Suddenly and unexpectedly, a young man in his late 20s shuffles along the aisle, mumbling to himself. He falls down, but stands up once again. He is unkempt; his face is bloodied. He tries to get people's attention, but many are repelled and move away or completely ignore him. But then, a middle-aged couple gets out of their seats to speak to him. They are shocked by the young man's condition and motion to the conductor to come over to them.

After speaking to the young man, the conductor calls out to all the people on the train. "Excuse me, ladies and gentleman, but I just wanted to show you what a real hero looks like. This man just risked his own life to save the life of an eight-year-old boy who dashed in front of this train. Please give him a round of applause!"

As you observed this scene, what was your first reaction when you found out that the man was a hero? Was this what you had thought of him? Had you been able to see beyond his appearance, or had you judged him? Could you sense something in your heart and feel love and compassion? In life, each one of us is at a different level of awareness and understanding. It is important not to judge others, for you never know a person's story until you walk in his or her shoes. Everyone has a worthwhile story. Be open. Respect one another. Listen to others with kindness and compassion.

7

LIVE YOUR TRUE LIFE

"I have found that the greatest degree of inner tranquility comes from the development of love and compassion. The more we care for the happiness of others, the greater our own sense of well-being becomes."

— TENZIN GYATSO, THE DALAI LAMA

How Can I Share the Energy of Love?

All souls originate from the same Source, but our Earth school affords us the opportunity to feel separate. This is a double-edged sword. Your nature is to be one with the whole, but as your awareness of your divine self diminishes, your ego takes over. This feeling of separation from our Source can manifest as the dark night of the soul.

Tiffany came to me many years ago wanting to get in touch with a long-lost friend. Tiffany was not a typical teenager because she seemed to do everything in her power *not* to conform. At 18, she'd left home to be on her own and spent her days Dumpster-diving to earn money to live. She would transform other people's trash into usable pieces of art and then sell her recycled goods online. She could not understand why people would discard items that were still useful. As Tiffany matured, she went through a series of relationships, but her drive, independence, and freethinking vision seemed to push men away. As a nonconformist, with pink dreadlocks, nose rings, and tattoos, Tiffany could not find work through the usual channels. She never held back her truth, and that seemed to ruffle everyone's feathers. Tiffany's life soon spiraled down into a solitary existence. Feeling lonely and unwanted, Tiffany began using drugs. It was her escape from the cruelties the world seemed to offer her. When she overdosed one night in an alley, she was carted off by ambulance into an emergency room. That was the moment when the life she had been living ended and another began.

As it happened, one of the emergency room doctors, Paul, had also been living a life of desperation. After he divorced his wife, he lost custody of his son and lived with his daughter, Pam. One night Pam took his car for a joyride with her friends. Everyone had been drinking. She lost control of the car and ran head-on into another vehicle, killing three people, including herself. Paul sank into guilt and self-loathing. That night in the emergency room was going to be his last. He had decided to give up medicine and drink himself to death.

The night that Tiffany was admitted to the emergency room, Paul recognized her immediately. She was one of Pam's classmates, and one of the few girls who had really known his daughter. It was kismet. Paul was determined to do everything he could to save her life. Two days later, when Tiffany woke from her coma, she saw Paul sitting beside her bed. He relayed all that had happened to her. Their friendship began, and as time went on, Tiffany became like a daughter to Paul. Paul changed his mind and stayed at the hospital so he could help Tiffany attend art school. After earning a master's degree, Tiffany became an advocate for sustainable lifestyles and now lectures at colleges around the country.

After Tiffany finished telling me her story, I began the reading, and her friend Pam, Paul's daughter, came through. Pam was very happy that her father had continued with his work and that he and Tiffany had such a strong bond. The whole reading was like a class reunion, because these three individuals had been together in other lifetimes, and would be together again to continue learning about love and compassion.

Solution: Compassion

Both Tiffany and Paul felt the illusion of separation that led to depression and despair. Through their compassion for each other's difficulties, they could share their light of awareness, and they were able to move beyond the illusion of separateness.

Compassion asks you to go within your heart and for a moment put yourself in another person's place. A compassionate heart empathizes with another person's pain. By helping each other stay positive and healthy, Tiffany and Paul were able to open themselves emotionally and share their love and concern for the other's well-being, Compassion brings people closer together. Like forgiveness, compassion is a gift for ourselves. When we take the time to forgive another and try to understand their situation or circumstances, we are putting compassion into action. As you make compassion a part of your daily life, you will begin to rewire your mind-set and to know how to do the right thing without hesitation. When we open ourselves up emotionally and link with another, we make their mind-set ours. The boundaries between us seem to fade. You feel the other person's suffering, and know what that suffering feels like. When I first began my work, I had to start seeing the world from many other points of view. It was an educational process, it taught me to be compassionate toward other people even if their lifestyles and beliefs were different from mine. By learning to be more compassionate, I grew strong in my desire to help alleviate suffering. By broadening my experiences, my thoughts changed as well, and I created a new mind-set. Compassion may be difficult for some at first, but once learned, it elevates the soul very quickly.

I demonstrate the language of my heart by
actively sharing and living loving acts.

Mindfulness—Living in the Now

As we become more aware of the power of love in ourselves, we begin to live a "mindful" life.

Mindfulness is living in the present moment and viewing the world from a larger perspective, one far beyond the little world of our egos. We are raised to look forward to the future and dwell on the past. This is part of our nature, and unfortunately, it is a mind-set that strips us of our power. Instead, we should be taught to learn from the past, live for today, and experience tomorrow. It is only when you are able to exist in the present moment while utilizing the energy of love and compassion that you can glimpse your true mission on Earth. When we are mindful, we are living in the moment when life is occurring. Only in the present can we respond to a situation. Will we make the most of it, or will we let it enslave us?

Instead of being caught up in fear and anticipation, we can press the pause button on our reactions to life's disturbances and see them as opportunities to use the power of love. Life is not a destination; it's a journey. In a world where everyone is "doing," we tend to miss the smaller and most significant parts of our learning experiences. We don't have to fast-forward every moment of life. Living in the moment teaches us that there is a time and place for everything.

As spiritual seekers, our goal is to practice mindfulness every day, in every hour of every day, and in every minute of every hour. It is easy to get caught up in social media, work, family, school, and chores and forget to take a moment to breathe and remind ourselves of who we really are. The mind (not the brain) is the soul. Spirit is constantly reminding us to stay present. Spending time thinking about what was or what will be only diminishes the potential we have right now. When we let go and exist in the present, we are able to bring the fullness of love to every thought and experience.

How Do I Demonstrate Confidence?

Living in the moment helps us to mature and progress as souls. With maturity comes confidence. A confident person has the ability not only to succeed but also, at the same time, to create an atmosphere that allows everyone on his or her path to prosper, learn, and grow.

When I first lived in Los Angeles, I didn't have a car and had to take the bus to work. At the time I was working in the basement of the William Morris Agency in Beverly Hills, pulling staples out of filed papers and preparing the pages for transfer to microfiche. (We didn't have scanning devices back then.) If you know anything about LA, you know buses are like foreign objects. One day during the rainy season, as I was standing in the rain at a bus stop, the street started to flood and my shoes went underwater. I thought, *That's it. I have to get a car.* My usual mantra was *I don't have enough money to get a car. I can't afford one.* But I decided to change my thinking around. Instead of *I can't*, I decided to visualize myself driving around LA in my beautiful sports car. Every day while waiting at the bus stop and then riding to work, I envisioned myself in that snazzy sports car.

Several months later, a friend asked if I would babysit his home while he was away on vacation in Hawaii. I jumped at the chance to live in his big house, even if only for a short time. After a few weeks, my friend called to tell me that he had decided to stay in Hawaii, and he asked if I could help him move. I was very happy to help make all the arrangements, pack up his home furnishings and personal items, and have them shipped. When it came time for me to send his car, he said, "You keep it for helping me." I was ecstatic. I ran to the garage and there it was—the car of my dreams. It had hundreds of thousands of miles on it, but I didn't care. It was an Alfa Romeo Spider convertible—my perfect car.

The more I had visualized what I wanted, the more optimistic I had become. When my friend asked me to mind his house, a window of opportunity opened. In helping my friend, I felt more self-assured of my capabilities. Receiving his car was icing on the cake. As my confidence strengthened, my determination to succeed also increased. After this incident, I was more open to the possibilities of giving and receiving. The Spider was just the beginning of many gifts. Not all were physical things. In time, my self-confidence helped me to trust in my ability to receive messages from Spirit.

I say everything works out as it should, but not always in the ways we expect. When things don't work out as you wish, don't abandon your dream. Use everything to learn and grow. If you are in the habit of second-guessing yourself all the time, you create inner conflict, which only leads to restlessness and anxiety. Your confidence is strained and weakened, and you act with hesitancy. Feeling unsure of yourself can bring little peace of mind. When you come from your center, you reside in your natural state of calm and inner knowing. This is real confidence. When your awareness is in the present moment, you are able to see a clearer path before you.

Solution: Expression

By directing your thoughts and words into action, you express your true soul character in whatever way that is. Let your soul's expression blossom and illuminate your ideas in tangible ways. There are many methods to demonstrate your individual soul expression, whether it is through words, art, movement, design, finances, education, and so on. I always thought my path would be as a comedy writer on a TV series. Little did I know 30 years ago that my expression in life would be to bring information from the Spirit world to help people remember that they are made of pure, unconditional love! When you're confident, you never try to be something that you're not. Remember that without you, the fullness of God's plan would be incomplete. You are a unique soul. Share your wisdom and expression. The world is waiting for you.

> I am ready to direct my words and
> transform them into ideas with love.

Staying in the Positive

Sometimes staying confident when your world is in chaos is a challenge. Many years ago, my good friend Carol had a mastectomy. When I spoke to her after her surgery, I was amazed by how well she was able to adapt to her changed body image. Although the loss of her feminine identity shattered her world for a while, she recognized that it gave her an opportunity to reflect on her priorities. Carol lived a luxurious lifestyle, but after the surgery, she said that she didn't take anything for granted anymore. "All the superficial niceties of life mean little to me now. Even the friends I used to have are gone," she revealed. "And I have stopped living someone else's expectations of who I am supposed to be and what I am supposed to look like." Carol changed her mind-set about a lot of things. The most important change was that she realized that she deserved love and that she had to be the first in line to love herself. Carol's surgery set her free to be herself. She was calm, confident, and looked forward to a new life ahead.

Our mind-body connection is always at work. When you accept that YOU ARE LOVE with all your heart, you will behave in ways that allow your life to flow with certainty and grace. You can start being more self-assured with positive affirmations. When you have a thought like *I'm sick and tired*, replace it with *I am worthwhile and always do my best*.

I use positive affirmations every day. I have one on my wall where I can see it all the time. Let the words sink into your heart and soul: *happy am I, healthy am I, holy am I*. Loving thoughts are health-giving in every aspect of your being, no matter what ailment, complaint, or obstacle comes your way.

Is It Possible to Love My Life?

More often than not, we are given spiritual gifts throughout our journeys in the physical realm. Sometimes we recognize these gifts, but often we take them for granted. Communicating with spirits has given me gifts of insight that I feel a desire to share with everyone I come in contact with. I cannot emphasize enough the importance of love in everything you do on the Earth plane. When you have confidence in yourself as a spiritual being, you will see everything in your life as a miracle and become aware of the many opportunities and possibilities available to you.

A few years back, I was a guest on the Fox syndicated TV series *The Morning Show with Mike and Juliet*. Both hosts were open and receptive to what I had to say, and I appreciated their kindness and cordiality. As soon as I sat down, I saw Mike's mother standing beside him and told him that she was around him most of the time, which was very gratifying to him. He told me that he and his mother had been very close and that he missed her very much.

After a few minutes, we turned our attention to the audience, and I was asked to do a reading for Kevin, a young man who had lost his mother when he was a boy. When I sat with him and his wife, Deena, my first impression was that his mother was sitting next to him. I began, "She gives you a kiss and love to the babies. She says she planned this meeting. She is also telling me you're going to have another baby. She protects your babies." Kevin and Deena were quite emotional as I was talking. I continued, "I'm seeing a country road, and your mother stands on the road looking around. This place is very rural. She is saying it's hard for you to go down that road."

Kevin explained to me that he and his mother had been driving down this road when a crop-duster plane crashed on top of their car, killing his mother. Kevin had been saved because she covered him when the plane landed on them. "She wants me to tell you not to care what other people think. It was not your fault." I told Kevin that his mom wanted to help him. "She is proud of you and wants you to get yourself going. You have had a hard life. You can do it. She's toasting you, if that makes any sense. She loves you very much. She's always with you and the kids." The love pouring out from his mother's words left Kevin in tears.

Kevin felt overwhelming guilt over his mother's tragic death. This kind of tragedy can have a self-defeating effect on a young boy, who isn't mature enough to understand that it wasn't his fault. He had turned to drugs and alcohol to alleviate his pain, but the pain never went away until that day with me, when he had closure with his mom and reexperienced her love again.

Kevin said, "I felt this wave [of guilt] completely leave me." His mother gave him love-filled reassurance that she would be around him whenever he needed her. Their soul-to-soul communication changed the way he looked at his life, stopped him from blaming himself, and replaced his guilt with confidence, wholeness, and happiness.

Years later, after finishing an event in Los Angeles, a man came up to me and asked, "Remember me?" I looked at him for a minute, then exclaimed, "Kevin!" We hugged as he thanked me for changing his life. Knowing that his mom was right there, watching over him and cheering him on, had relieved him of his burden of grief and blame. Kevin found his confidence, as well as a career that he loved. "I have a good life now. My mother would be very proud of me, I know," he said. He then whispered into my ear in the sweetest of ways, "I even know it was her that pulled some strings to get me a better job than the one I had!"

Solution: Satisfaction

Kevin had struggled to find his self worth, but once he released his guilt and heard the reassuring advice of his mother, he felt confident enough to go on with his life. When you accept yourself, you confirm to the Universe that you are everything you are meant to be, shortcomings and all. You can live your life and make choices out of love rather than fear. Your soul is absolutely perfect; your ego is inherently insecure. One of the ego's biggest traps is dissatisfaction. The ego is always judging, and its criticism fills our minds with doubt and indecision. It is never content with what it has; it is always searching for the next "better" thing. We have to look past all appearances and recognize the truth. You aren't meant to be someone else, so don't compare yourself to someone else. You are on a journey of self-discovery. Be true to yourself, and you will be content with your life.

I let the energy of love guide me so that
I no longer need others to define who I am.

MEDITATION—EXPRESSION

Imagine yourself standing in front of a blank canvas. You are about to express your soul self on this canvas by channeling the "higher aspects" of your being. As you begin, all the items you need to paint appear: an easel to put your canvas on, brushes of various shapes and sizes, a palette on which to mix your colors, and assorted jars of color.

Picture yourself picking up a paintbrush and beginning to paint your life in color and design. Every thought you have ever had has been imbued with a certain color and texture. With each stroke of the brush, the color of a thought appears, matching very closely to an emotion.

As you create your painting, see how the colors and the design change from your childhood to your teenage years and finally into adulthood. Be cognizant of how your soul self portrays the influential people on your journey. What are the colors influencing these particular people? Do they blend with the rest of the painting, or do they clash with your colors, making the painting discordant and unbalanced? Because this painting represents your soul self, it clearly illustrates the love or the fear in your life. You can tell by the colors—light and vibrant colors show love, compassion, and joy, while dark and murky colors depict fear, limitation, and living someone else's life instead of your own.

Remember that this painting is a tool for self-expression and is guided by the intentions and integral choices that have shaped your life. As you view the painting before you, what colors or design do you think you will use to complete it? What, if anything, is missing? Now is your opportunity to enhance your life experience by seeing the color of love begin to fill the empty spaces on your canvas. You can return to this canvas anytime you feel the need to express your soul self and refine the colors and reshape the design.

8

MOVING FORWARD

"The biggest advances are not made by being a great teacher; they are made by being a great student."

— GARY R. RENARD, *THE DISAPPEARANCE OF THE UNIVERSE*

Manifest the Power of Love Daily

Love has so much to teach us. It is through others that we learn to love the most. When we allow ourselves to be a part of someone's life, the "boundaries" we once imagined seem to fade. As we commit to a life of love, we will grow in a willingness to learn and accept from one another. To manifest more love, find a support group of friends or like-minded individuals with whom you can share your experiences. As you share with others, you will find that everyone is really the same.

Another way to bring more love into your life is by writing your thoughts and feelings in a journal every day. Let your soul self write to your Earth self. It is a good way to clear your mind and help you focus on the attributes and goals that are right for you. Another way to transform yourself is by taking the high road of kindness and forgiveness with everyone you meet. Give generously to others by offering uplifting words, smiles, and caring. Encourage family and friends to be themselves and to be courteous and thoughtful in their treatment of others.

When you share this kind of energy, it has a ripple effect. You will begin to feel more peaceful and relaxed. Realize that while you are changing, your soul is always connected to the source of love within and without. This simple shift in your awareness will help to shine a little light on everyone with whom you come into contact.

How Can I Make the World a Place
I Would Like to Live In?

During a demonstration in Minneapolis a few years back, a young man came through from Spirit to communicate with his parents in the audience. This in itself was not unusual, but the content of the message was quite incredible. Each person in attendance was reminded of the importance of open-mindedness.

The young man who had passed, Matthew, thanked his father and mother for coming there that night. He was sorry for the things he had said to them before his death. Both parents were visibly shaken by receiving their son's forgiveness and love. As the reading went on, they explained that their son had died of AIDS. "We assumed he got the disease through homosexual activities," said the mother. "Because our church doesn't condone this behavior, we did not speak to him until just before his death." There were some rumbles of disapproval from the audience. I quieted everyone down. "We're not here to judge each other," I said to the audience. Then Matthew continued with his communication. He relayed that he wished he had had a different relationship with his parents, but that he understood where they were coming from. His parents began to cry. They explained that they had been holding on to guilt and remorse for so long that it had begun to destroy their health. They knew that if they had not been so ignorant and closed-minded, they could have helped their son get through his illness. "Your son forgives you both. He doesn't want you to suffer. Please let it go, he says," I told them.

At that moment, a young woman in the audience stood up and interrupted the reading. She turned to Matthew's parents and introduced herself as Michelle. She apologized to me and the audience for interrupting, but she had realized during the reading that she had known Matthew. "Matthew wasn't gay. We dated each other for several months. Matthew dealt with a drug addiction that I helped him get intervention for, but he contracted AIDS by using dirty needles. I knew that he was HIV-positive and he understood that you assumed he was gay. And he let you assume that because he thought you'd be more accepting of that than the real reason he had contracted the virus: he had been experimenting with heroin." Not only were Matthew's parents dumbfounded, but so was everyone in the audience, including me. "We were planning to get married when we had enough money saved."

At the end of the evening, Matthew's parents and Michelle came backstage. "We can't thank you enough for bringing Matthew to us," said the mother. "Your son wanted you to heal your regret," I answered. Matthew's father said, "After our son died, we realized that we had to change things at our church. We sponsored a workshop on diversification for our church members with an emphasis on outreach to the gay community. Matthew's death provided the impetus for us to see that we needed to be open to different cultures and ways of life."

We all couldn't help but chuckle at the mysterious ways that Spirit works. Matthew's parents had taken a tragedy and turned it into a positive. The regret that they had felt over their "gay" son prompted them to change the hearts and minds of others in their church—and only now were they discovering that their son was heterosexual but had used a dirty needle. Michelle confirmed that Matthew had been clean and sober when they met, but said he was so ashamed of his drug use that he never dissuaded his parents from presuming his sexuality.

Several years later, I received a letter from Michelle. She wrote that she and Matthew's parents were still in contact and that Matthew's father had recently had a heart transplant. "The donor was a twenty-four-year-old gay man. Ironic, isn't it?" she said.

Solution: Tolerance

Sometimes this school called Earth can be a very daunting destination, and our lessons can be staggering. Matthew's parents had lost not only their child but also their compassion over what they thought was an unacceptable lifestyle. They are not alone in their narrow-mindedness. The lesson for them and for many is tolerance. Souls who graduate with high honors from Earth school are the ones who can see past the illusions of race, gender, sexuality, and religion. As the Bible says, "Love thy neighbor as thyself." We come here in many guises, but they are merely false appearances that only seem real. We all emanate from the One Source. When you have tolerance, you are secure within your own sense of self. You are not swayed by the prejudices of someone else or a group or society. You appreciate your fellow travelers, and no matter what their points of view, you treat them all with respect.

> I appreciate other points of view because
> I sense the love in everyone.

Can I See the Energetic Life Force in Everything?

Although many of our lessons come from human relationships, we cannot forget that there is a life force in every living thing on our planet and everything has an effect on us. One must be willing to adapt to changing conditions and situations. No one is too old to learn or change, and you must be willing to see each day as a new opportunity for discovery. Don't close off your good by being unwilling to experience new things. Life is going on all around us whether we can visibly see it or not.

I was teaching a class in La Jolla, California, to beginning and intermediate mediums who were looking to further their links with the Spirit world. We were discussing intuition and opening ourselves to the still, small voice within. During the class, Donna, one of the students, recalled an incident with her cat.

"I had a rescue cat; his name was Binky. The person who had him was dying of cancer," she began. "He was a very large orange tabby, and as soon as I brought him home, he laid in the middle of the kitchen floor as if he'd always belonged there." She went on to describe how the cat was very friendly to all the stray cats in the neighborhood, even going as far as sharing his bowl of food with them. "One day,

I found Binky on the bed, and he wasn't moving." Donna immediately scooped him up and took him to the emergency vet. "He had heart failure, so they put him into an oxygen cage to see if he could live through the night." The vet told Donna that her cat had a very slim chance of surviving. She explained, "I was told that if Binky survived, he would last at most another six months." But her cat did survive the six months, and in fact went on to live another seven years. "Binky was so spiritual—he taught me a lot about sharing love."

The day arrived when Binky was too sick to survive, and Donna brought him to the vet to be euthanized. "It was his time, and it was very hard for me." As Donna sat with her cat in the small exam room, she said her good-byes. She continued, "As soon as the vet gave Binky the shot, he was gone. Suddenly, I had a vision. The door to the room swung open, and a lovely woman in a long, flowery gown floated in. She looked like a Greek goddess. Around her were little animals, like rabbits, dogs, squirrels, and birds. Then I saw Binky's spirit jump off the vet's table and follow the goddess and the other animals out the door, into a garden filled with golden light. I knew that he was going home." Needless to say, by the end of the story there wasn't a dry eye in the classroom. Everyone who had ever had a pet related to this wonderful example showing that the souls of all living beings return to heaven.

Many of us are fortunate to see energies around people, animals, plants, and water. But if you can't see them, allow yourself some time to sense them through your intuition. We all possess intuition—it is our sixth sense. Everyone's sense of intuition is different and colored by life experiences. By opening yourself to your inner voice, you allow your soul to guide you through any experience.

All the elements of the natural world, including animals, flowers, trees, and so on, can create a communal feeling of oneness. The more we tap in to our intuition in the way that Donna did with her cat, the more we develop an innate awareness of our surroundings, and the more love will grow within our hearts.

Solution: Transformation

Just as a caterpillar eventually becomes a butterfly, you, too, are slowly awakening to your true heritage as a spiritual being. As you go through this awakening, others will see your light and feel your love, and your love will expand. Our soul-to-soul connection, whether it is with another human, an animal, or nature, magnifies our vibration, allowing transformation to happen more quickly. As it says in *A Course in Miracles*, "What you perceive in others you are strengthening in yourself." As you advance into a new insight of yourself, you may lose attachment to material things, family, career, and even yourself. Your relationships with others may change as your awareness shifts from human to spiritual. You will come to understand that you are a part of a grand scheme of life, and that your place in the Universe contributes to the whole.

> I use the power of love to move
> through illusions and shift my awareness.

MEDITATION—TRANSFORMATION

This is the time to remember your Source. You are the essence of the heavens above and will always be a part of the materials from which the heavens are made. As you focus on your breath, concentrate on your heart space. With every inhalation, see yourself growing and expanding upward and outward in all directions. Don't be afraid. You are much more than your body.

See yourself connecting with the sky, sun, moon, and galaxies. The stars are your doorways to the light dimensions. Begin to connect with the light world around you. After several breaths, in your mind's eye, scan the galaxy and find a star that has your name and energy. When you find the star, become one with its light and its exquisite energy. Step inside it and feel its healing properties transforming you. You are becoming one with this light energy. Become aware of any dense or destructive energy you have been holding on to, and see it suddenly drop off you. The power and energy of love now fills in the space. As it does, you become lighter, and you float higher into the heavens with light energy.

When you are true to the magnificence of your soul, you are open to receive healing. The Universe always provides whatever you need. Become aware that you are much more than what you think and feel. You are a soul being beyond human comprehension; your soul light endures through eternity. The power of love not only transforms your soul but also contributes more to the world than you'll ever know.

9

THE
DOORWAY
HOME

"I am a spark from the Infinite.
I am not flesh and bones. I am light."

— Paramahansa Yogananda, *Metaphysical Meditations*

Life Review

When we leave the physical plane and enter the heavenly dimensions, we will know that we are home, where we truly belong. The first thing we will experience is a life review. You cannot hide your thoughts in heaven because it is a mental realm. You will get to look back at your life and be your own judge and jury. You will experience what you created. If you were hurtful or unkind, you will relive the words and actions over and over until you can forgive yourself. That is why I teach people to be responsible now for their thoughts, words, and deeds, because all will be waiting for us on the other side. Learn now to have patience, be forgiving, and live with love and compassion for each person that comes upon your path.

People often ask me if after a period of time spirits move on and no longer stay around us. I explain that spirits are not like us; they are not linear beings constrained by time. There is no *time* in the Spirit realms; gravity and time are attributes of Earth. A soul can be in many dimensions, including the Earth plane, at the same "time." Yes, spirits do move on to other dimensions, but they are always around if we ask for their help and will do what they can to support us.

How Can I Bridge Heaven and Earth?

In traveling the world over, I am always amazed and inspired along with my audiences by the amount of love that comes through from spirit people. The messages I receive are ones in which spirits always feel love toward the ones they leave behind. They convey that they are alive and happy and ask that the living not cry over them anymore. They describe floating up to the other side and seeing golden lights as they pass through the heavenly dimensions. They realize that these golden lights are other souls waiting for them. There is a joyful reunion among spirits as they join their soul groups in the oneness of this beautiful golden light.

Many years ago I was in Palm Springs, California, for a demonstration at one of the local casinos. I received a call from my friend Anne, whose mother, Rose, was in a hospice in Palm Desert. She asked if I would visit, and of course I said yes. When I arrived at the hospice, I noticed how quiet it was—a pleasant place to make a life transition, I thought. Anne greeted me and I could see the worry on her face. I squeezed her hand and said, "Don't be afraid." When we arrived at her mother's room, I saw a small, frail woman in the bed by the window. Her eyes were closed and she looked peaceful, much more peaceful than my friend did. A crucifix stood on the nightstand, along with rosary beads and a Bible. The priest had already been there to give her the last rites.

I closed my eyes and said a prayer to ask for guidance, and when I opened them I saw a small, round spirit woman sitting on Rose's right side at the head of the bed. I turned to Anne and told her what I saw. "It sounds like my grandmother. My mother and she were very close." The little round woman didn't say anything; it was as if she had been waiting patiently for this moment to arrive, when she would be reunited with her dearest daughter. As I looked around, the room began to fill up with a large group of spirit people, all with various values of color and light. I knew Rose would be leaving very shortly to go back to her spiritual home. "Your mother has a lot of people waiting for her. She is very loved." Anne half smiled and half cried as she spoke: "She came from a big family of eleven brothers and sisters. I suppose everyone is waiting for her, as she is the last one to go. I know she loved them very much and missed them all."

Then suddenly I felt something brush past me and touch the back of my head. I could feel my hair fly up. At that moment, Rose took her last breath. I saw a luminous being that looked very much like an angel take Rose's spirit body by the hand and lead her toward the waiting crowd. It was a phenomenal sight. As I explained what I was seeing to Anne, she began crying. "Your mother is alive," I whispered. "She's very happy; she is with her family, and they are guiding her back home." Rose's family and friends greeted her with the love she had shared with them over life-times. The whole room felt lighter and brighter than when I first walked in. As the nurse stepped into the room, I gave my friend a hug good-bye.

Rose's passing was another validation from the Spirit world that no one ever dies alone. It is a party, a welcoming, and a moment that all have been waiting for. This reminds me of a wonderful insight—that when we are born, we cry, and others are happy; when we die, others cry, and we are happy. The only thing we take when we leave this Earth is the love we gave and the love we received.

Solution: Joy

When I can give a message of love and comfort from the Spirit world to a workshop attendee, a TV guest, a radio caller, or a friend, I receive tremendous joy. Being in a position to relieve a grieving heart and share the bonds of eternal love is one of the greatest blessings of my life. Seeing the love and beauty around Rose as she moved toward her waiting family and friends gave me an incredible sense of joy. I knew that the love Rose had when she was alive was the love she was bringing with her. I was happy to help my friend, and in time, I knew that Anne would feel at peace with her mother's passing, and would be reunited with her one day.

A state of joy comes from living in happiness, grace, and gratitude. When you become aware of the abundance you have, without comparison and regret, then you can serve others. Joy comes through you and reaches everyone you encounter. You celebrate life and delight in it. The joy you share fills your soul, and you feel fulfilled. Like love, joy crosses into all dimensions and bridges the Spirit world with our human world.

The ancient Egyptians believed they would be asked two questions upon death. The first: Did you bring joy? The second: Did you find joy? When you are in tune with the vibration of joy, you are content, serene, and able to move forward through life's struggles with optimism, spreading your good cheer to all.

> I delight in the love of life and
> share my love in all that I do.

How Can I Connect to the Essence of Oneness?

I had an experience several years ago that blew my mind. I brought a group of about 30 people to Sedona, Arizona, on a UFO expedition as part of a spiritual sojourn. Sedona is known for its vortexes of energy, supposedly due to the ore and minerals buried deep in the ground. It was a Saturday around 10 P.M. when the group and I reached the top of Boynton Canyon to await a connection with the Star people from other galaxies. After staring at the clear starlit sky for a while, I became frustrated. Nothing was happening. I knew the folks wanted some kind of experience. Suddenly I heard one of my spirit guides saying very clearly in my mind, *You must meditate to raise the vibrations and tune in to the frequencies of a higher calling.* I turned to the group and shared my guide's advice, and we all sat quietly as I led the group in a guided meditation. Just minutes later, everyone began to see colored lights in the sky. A local tour guide approached and said, "They're here. Can you communicate with them?"

I walked into the middle of a field and opened my chakra points. Chakras are pools of energy that spin together to form the body's energy system. There are seven chakra points from the root to the crown. Each chakra corresponds to a color and generates energy for a different part of the body. When a chakra is blocked by any kind of emotional upset, mental burnout, or physical trauma, it needs to be unblocked or energized. By directing breath, color, visualization, and emotional self-awareness at each chakra point, like a flower, it begins to open. For example, the first or root chakra spins at the base of the spine and has to do with the survival instinct and basic physical needs. A lot of fear can block this chakra and sap the body of vitality. Breathing the color red into this area will help to bring the fear to the surface. Once the fear is realized, it can be surrendered and the chakra point can open, much like a flower opening to the sun.

As I visualized my chakra points opening, it suddenly became crystal clear that the energy surrounding me had changed. I knew the Star people were attempting to slow down their frequencies so that I could hear them. A few seconds passed. Then I felt the most incredible loving presence. The words I heard in my mind were strong, yet I knew these beings had to slow them down so that I was able to comprehend them. I heard: *We are from the Pleiades. There is one thing we don't understand about the human race. You have the energy of love all around you, yet you choose not to use it. Why?*

This moving experience had a tremendous effect on the entire group, especially me. Not only did we experience a civilization far greater than we had ever known but we also realized that love encompasses the far reaches of the Universe. The message confirmed that love is everywhere. To me, human intelligence is still in the "child" stage because many of us on Earth are young souls. Unlike the more advanced souls beyond our world, we cannot see the shining light of love within or around us.

I don't believe it's possible to comprehend the mysteries of existence with the human brain. Our brains are finite and limited, like our physical bodies, and one day will cease to exist. But our minds, which are part and parcel of our souls, live on in a reality we cannot yet fathom. Our souls gravitate to a level in Spirit that is based on the love we have expressed during our lifetimes. The more I do my work, the stronger my belief is that a single thought or act of love that you can perform right now will affect past-life experiences and future-life experiences. I can only encourage you to think about love—all the ways you push it away, and all the ways you can experience more of it. Begin to use it now.

Solution: Unity

The power of love unifies the worlds within worlds, those we see and those we don't see. The love we share with one another is amplified and travels beyond the physical dimension into planes of existence far beyond our capacity to understand. When you love yourself and others, the energy of love is returned and magnified. Whether the soul is another human, an animal, or a loved one who has passed into Spirit, love never dies. It is an eternal, unbroken bond, the connecting force that is changeless, timeless, and joins us together forever. As my friend Violette said to me from the other side, "We are never alone when we feel another's love." Eventually, each of us will be reunited in the divine love and light. Not one soul is ever lost.

> I understand that the love
> I share with another is love amplified.

MEDITATION—JOY

Close your eyes and focus on your breathing. With each inhalation, energize the space around your heart. Send out an intention or thought to the Universe for healing. Say, *I release all tension, stress, and pain so that I can be healed.* As you send out the thought, release any situation, person, or mind conditioning that has caused you to feel anxiety or pain. The past is over, so there is no need to hold on to it. The future is yet to be, so there is nothing you need to do. All you truly have is this present moment. As you continue to breathe, listen to your heartbeat. With each beat, align yourself with present-moment awareness. The only thing of importance in this present moment is the essence of your soul, which is love and joy.

If it is difficult for you to be in the present moment, ask yourself, *Am I making choices with joy and lightness?* If not, you may perceive life as a struggle. Focus again on your heartbeat and honor the present moment. As you relax, let all unhappiness and all circumstances that suppress your joy vanish. Welcome the present moment and be open to joy. It is only when you are able to feel joy that the power of love works easily and effortlessly.

When your soul nature is balanced and harmonious with joy, you will be at peace and feel connected to all of life.

AFTERWORD

Only Love Is Real

There are only two illusions that we think are real. The first illusion is separateness. When we are in Spirit, we are one; there is no separation. Only on Earth do we feel cut off from one another. We are energy beings. On the dense, heavy Earth plane, our energy vibrates at a very slow rate and we appear to be solid. In the Spirit world of golden light, souls vibrate at a much higher frequency; they appear as pure light. While spirits may seem invisible to us, believe me, they are around us all the time.

The second one is death. Because we fear the unknown, death is the greatest of all our fears because it is the greatest unknown. I am often asked whether I am afraid of death. My answer is *no* because there is no death; there is a transformation from a physical dimension to a heavenly dimension. I look forward to the day when my work here in the Earth school is finished and I can join my loved ones, soul mates, and guides once again. Until that time, I live every moment as best I can and treat everyone the best that I can.

The more knowledge we have, the less fear we will have. When we are in complete alignment with the power of love, we will realize that death is merely an illusion. Only love is real.

Love,

James

ABOUT THE AUTHOR

© Michael Amico

James Van Praagh is hailed throughout the world as a pioneer of the mediumship movement and is recognized as one of the most accurate spiritual mediums working today. He is the internationally renowned #1 *New York Times* bestselling author of *Talking to Heaven, Reaching to Heaven, Healing Grief, Heaven and Earth, Looking Beyond, Meditations, Ghosts Among Us, Unfinished Business, Growing Up in Heaven, Adventures of the Soul* and *How to Heal a Grieving Heart* (co-authored with Doreen Virtue). His messages have brought solace, peace and spiritual insights, changing millions' view of both life and death. He has received many awards for his dedication to raising the consciousness of the planet.

James recently launched The James Van Praagh School of Mystical Arts, a labour of love that was years in the making. The online school offers a variety of learning experiences, from professional certifications to audio and video courses, with live calls and online forums.

Fans of James can tune in to his popular Hay House Radio show, *Talking to Spirit*, every Tuesday at 11:00 A.M. Pacific, and enjoy his online television series, *Spirit Talk*, on Gaia.com. He also shares insights and messages from the Spirit realm through his website and via social media.

www.vanpraagh.com

Hay House Titles of Related Interest

YOU CAN HEAL YOUR LIFE, the movie, starring Louise Hay
& Friends (available as a 1-DVD program and an expanded
2-DVD set) Watch the trailer at: www.LouiseHayMovie.com

THE SHIFT, the movie, starring Dr. Wayne W. Dyer (available
as a 1-DVD program and an expanded 2-DVD set) Watch the
trailer at: www.DyerMovie.com

LIFE LOVES YOU: 7 Spiritual Practices to Heal Your Life,
by Louise Hay and Robert Holden

LOVE HAS FORGOTTEN NO ONE: The Answer to Life,
by Gary R. Renard

THE TOP TEN THINGS DEAD PEOPLE WANT TO TELL YOU,
by Mike Dooley

TUNE IN: Let Your Intuition Guide You to Fulfillment and Flow,
by Sonia Choquette

All of the above are available at www.hayhouse.co.uk

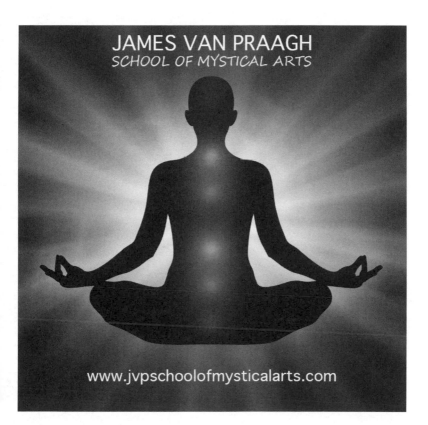

JAMES VAN PRAAGH
SCHOOL OF MYSTICAL ARTS

www.jvpschoolofmysticalarts.com

NOTES

NOTES

NOTES

NOTES

HAY HOUSE

Look within

Join the conversation about latest products,
events, exclusive offers and more.

f Hay House UK

🐦 @HayHouseUK

📷 @hayhouseuk

❤ healyourlife.com

We'd love to hear from you!